Living Maya

Living Maya

Text by Walter F. Morris, Jr.

Photographs by Jeffrey J. Foxx

Harry N. Abrams, Inc., Publishers

Editor: Beverly Fazio
Designer: Michael Hentges

Library of Congress Cataloging-In-Publication Data
Morris, Walter F., Jr.
  Living Maya
  1. Mayas. I. Foxx, Jeffery Jay. II. Title.
F1435.M765 1987 972.81'01   87–1415
ISBN 0–8109–2745–4 (pbk.)

Photographs on pages 38, 127, 182 by Christiana Dittmann
Textiles in the Picture Essay "Woven Clouds" are from the Sna
Jolobil Weavers' Collection

Paperback edition published in 2000 by Harry N. Abrams,
Incorporated, New York

Clothbound edition published in 1987 by Harry N. Abrams,
Incorporated, New York

Printed and bound in Japan

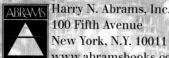

Harry N. Abrams, Inc.
100 Fifth Avenue
New York, N.Y. 10011
www.abramsbooks.com

PAGE 1: Rosha Hernandez, the master weaver of San Andres Larráinzar, wearing a ceremonial *huipil*.

PAGES 2–3: A family compound in the Chiapas Highlands. Family
members build separate houses adjacent to their cornfields but
share a long cookhouse such as the one seen at the left.

PAGES 4–5: Having carried the sack of cabbages with a tumpline
from his home in an outlying hamlet, a Chamula man waits at the
side of the road for a truck to take him to market in the town center.

THESE PAGES: Floating through the open weave of Carranza cloth,
the silken threads of the brocade form geometric designs to symbolize snakes and "V"-shaped fish bones.

Contents

Introduction: Chiapas   9

The Maya in Time   19

    Picture Essay: The Highlands   36

At Home   61

    Picture Essay: The Lord's Work   72

Daughters of the Earthlord   105

    Picture Essay: Woven Clouds   120

The Ancesters' Dreams   153

The Saints' Day   165

    Picture Essay: Celebrating the Demon's Defeat   176

Epilogue   209

Selected Bibliography   214

Illustration Credits   215

    Picture Essay: As It Was in the Beginning   216

Acknowledgments   224

Introduction:
Chiapas

The Highlands of Chiapas rise sharp and isolate above the tropics. At night the stars shine close and cold, and at dawn fog surrounds the sacred mountains and steep cornfields. As the sun rises, the volcanic peaks loom above the clouds like islands dreaming of the sea. Within each mountain dwells an Earthlord, the mythical being who directs the clouds, the rain, and the riches of the earth.

Just below the summit of Moss Mountain, the most sacred mountain of the Highlands, three cross shrines mark the entrance to three small caves. Crosses are gateways to the Earthlord's subterranean domain. Every May shamans and religious officials arrive with fireworks and music to celebrate the beginning of the rainy season. After cleaning the shrines, giving the wooden crosses a new bloom of flowers, and offering prayers, songs, and shots of sugarcane rum to the Earthlord and to the saints in heaven, the celebrants climb the last few yards to the summit to visit the television repeating station there and to have a drink with the technicians. After all, both shamans and technicians are in the business of maintaining culture. Each, of course, is secretly certain that the other is a fool, but both enjoy this yearly meeting on high.

The Maya are familiar with television, cars, radios, airplanes, and other wonders of Western civilization, which they use, as do most of us, without fully understanding. We, unfortunately, are almost completely ignorant of Maya civilization, one of the most remarkable cultures of the Americas. The Maya were writing books in a phonetic script fifteen hundred years before Columbus discovered the New World. The corn, beans, and squash that we eat were first cultivated by the Maya and their neighbors. Basic mathematical concepts such as zero and place numbers were being used in Maya astronomical calculations of eclipse cycles while the West was still stumbling along with Roman numerals. Two thousand years ago Maya craftsmen were building pyramids and palaces without metal

OPPOSITE: One of three shrines to the Holy Ancestors on the hills around Chamula center. The Ancestors are the supernatural elders of each community; they watch over their people, punishing those who deviate from tradition, and teach shamans how to restore the well-being of lost souls.

tools. Between the cities, through impenetrable swamps and jungles, they laid out long, white roads that served as platforms for royal processions. Yet the Maya never tamed beasts of burden, and they used the wheel only for toys. The Maya created the most advanced civilization in the New World with a technology that was neolithic.

Although many scholarly studies seem to treat Maya civilization as one of history's closed chapters, the Maya did not vanish. Almost one million Maya-speaking people live in Chiapas, the southernmost state of Mexico, and another three million live in Yucatán, Belize, Guatemala, Honduras, and El Salvador.

Despite the fact that they are familiar with the machines and life-style of modern civilization, or perhaps because they do know the alternatives, the people of the Chiapas Highlands are extremely conservative. The food they eat, the way it is prepared, the stories, myths, and dreams they tell while dipping a tortilla into a bowl of beans, the festivals they celebrate each season of the year are all parts of a tradition that the Maya say God gave to them "at the beginning of the world." Although Maya men may work and travel throughout Chiapas, the Highlands are their cultural home.

Across the mountains lies a quiltwork of communities, each slightly different from its close neighbors. There are four distinct Maya languages spoken in the Highlands. Tzotzil Maya speakers inhabit the western Highlands, Tzeltal Maya occupy the eastern slopes leading toward the Lacandon jungle. In the cloud forests above the Classic Maya ruins of Palenque dwell the Chol Maya, and to the south, toward the border with Guatemala, live Tojolobal Maya. Each of these language groups is further divided into communities, some fifty in the Highlands alone, whose members speak a particular dialect of the language, wear a distinct style of dress, worship a special patron saint, and consider all members of the community as relatives. The populations of Highland

communities average about twenty thousand inhabitants. Chamula is the largest, with over one hundred thousand people, and many communities have only a few thousand. Each community has its own government and courts, in which local judges try all cases except those concerning crimes of murder. The church, government buildings, and market occupy the community center. Few people have homes there. The houses in the center provide temporary quarters for the civil and religious officials, who give a year's service to the community. Most people live in small hamlets scattered throughout the surrounding hills. During markets and festivals they crowd the center to trade, celebrate, and meet with friends. More than a political and religious entity, a Maya community is like an immense extended family.

When I arrived in Chiapas in 1972, after traveling through the Highlands, I was invited to live with Mol Sanate's family in the community of San Andrés Larráinzar. Mol Sanate was, and still is, the sage and clown of the community. Every Sunday, every feast day, the old man walks an hour to the center to discuss politics with the elders in the town hall and to drink with the religious officials in front of the church. Greeting each friend with a few words, joking, and occasionally getting outrageously drunk, as is his right as an elder, Mol Sanate appears to be just another man having a good time on his day off. But during all his interactions, Mol Sanate is taking the pulse of the community—listening to gossip, making sure that the married couples who serve the saints that year complete their tasks of preparation and prayer, forging a consensus between the elders and the young educated men about who should be the next mayor.

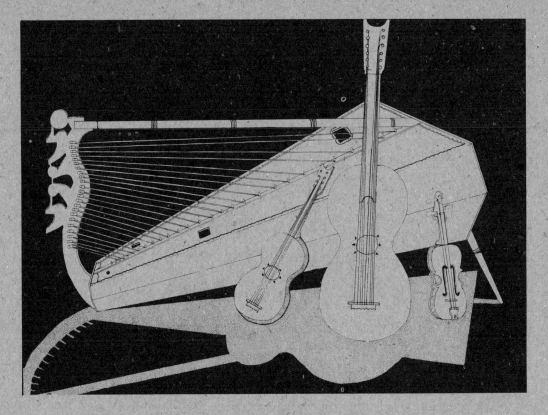

At home Mol Sanate never drinks and never receives visitors. He and his two sons own enough land to grow all their corn and vegetables. They have a small pasture for a cow and horse; pigs root under the apple trees, and a flock of brown chickens scratch in the patio. By San Andrés standards Mol is a wealthy man. His only commercial venture is the making and selling of fireworks for festivals. He grows cane for the casings of the skyrockets, reeds for the sticks, and maguey for the rope that binds them together. Since charcoal is abundant, the only item he purchases for making gunpowder is saltpeter. In fact, he buys almost nothing, only a new hoe or machete once a decade. The only thing he ever asked me to buy for him was a file to sharpen his tools. I bring him one every year as tribute.

In his house I learned to speak Tzotzil. The Maya call their language *Batz'i K'op*, "True Speech." Tzotzil is rich in puns, with a complex grammar and a few odd sounds—glottal stops, for instance, the pause in the flow of air just after sounding a vowel, as occurs in English between the two syllables in "oh-oh." Every vowel in Tzotzil can be glottalized, thus giving the sound a different meaning. Consonants in Tzotzil can be aspirated, and these sudden explosive sounds also alter meaning. A *chuch* is a squirrel, but a *ch'uch'* is a frog.

Tzotzil would have been very difficult for me to learn had I not had a wonderful teacher, Mol Sanate's three-year-old grandson, called Melon because of his round head. Every day I would practice pronouncing the words I had heard while Melon rolled on the grass, laughing. Melon was learning Tzotzil much faster than I and loved teasing me with his superior vocabulary. After a year I could converse with any grown-up in San Andrés. By then I had become fascinated with another kind of language: the ancient symbols woven into Maya costumes.

Women weave most of the clothing for their families. They add a striped pattern or a few designs to their husband's shirts and belts. The large rectangular blouses, called *huipiles*, that Highland women wear are warm and beautiful and bear elaborate geometric designs that describe the Maya cosmos. The sun's course through thirteen layers of the sky and underworld and the creation of clouds by the Earthlord with the help of his servants, the toads and snakes, are composed in a harmony that entices the earth to flower. Weavers capture that moment when the world is renewed.

Chiapas is a young land, alive with volcanoes and earthquakes, yet each stone, each patch of ground carries signs of generations of people who have worked the earth into a habitable place for humankind. Unlike the many other peoples of the Americas who have migrated from place to place, the Maya have weathered cycles of decline and rebirth in the same fractured land for four thousand years.

The oldest excavated Maya settlement, Cuello, in Belize, dates to 2500 B.C. Early villagers apparently enjoyed an egalitarian society: they built neither sumptuous tombs nor great temples. During what archaeologists call the Formative period (1500–100 B.C.) the Maya probably lived much as their descendants do today. Farmers cultivated corn, a plant first

Pre-Columbian Maya corn god

domesticated in Mexico around 5000 B.C., and eventually learned to grow abundant crops in the dry limestone soil of Yucatán, in raised fields along flooding tropical rivers, and on the steep mountain slopes of Guatemala and Chiapas.

Though increasingly prosperous, the Maya people avoided trade with the more advanced cultures around them. The Olmecs had established great artistic and theocratic centers on the Gulf Coast between 1200 and 600 B.C., and the Mixtecs of Oaxaca had developed a rudimentary form of writing by 400

B.C.; yet the Maya remained a comparatively simple agricultural society. Then, around 100 B.C., Maya culture was mysteriously, inexplicably transformed. Small villages suddenly exploded into large urban centers ruled by a powerful elite. At Mirador, in Guatemala, enormous pyramids that rivaled those of Teotihuacán in the Valley of Mexico were erected in a single generation. During the pre-Classic period, from 100 B.C. to A.D. 200, the Maya adopted ideas from cultures they had previously ignored. Under a new and dynamic nobility they perfected the calendar and hieroglyphic writing to express their own concepts and record their own history.

Classic Maya culture (A.D. 200–900) achieved a new equilibrium in government and a sublime grace in the arts. The richly costumed figures carved on stone monuments or stelae are portraits of kings performing sacrificial rites that sustained the gods. The complex hieroglyphic texts alongside each scene reveal the name and titles of the ruler, when he ruled, and how he descended from the gods, as Maya kings were believed to be divine. At the height of the Classic period, hundreds of divine kings ruled hundreds of city-states. Some dominated their neighbors to form small kingdoms, but no center ever arose to unite the independent and often antagonistic Maya states into a single empire.

In a small temple at Bonampak, a site in the Chiapas rain forest, lavish murals depict the violent rituals held in behalf of the royal heir. Drums and trumpets play while actors masked as sea creatures dance for their new lord and god. The murals go on to show the assembled nobles raiding a neighboring town, capturing its king, and sacrificing him to assure the divinity of their prince. The boy never ascended to the throne, however, for Bonampak itself was attacked soon after and destroyed. The last paintings have moldered, and the temples, like countless others, have surrendered to the forest.

The fall of Classic Maya civilization ended a thousand years of relative stability. One by one lowland

Chaan-Muan, the Lord of Bonampak, being dressed for the ceremonial designation of his heir

cities such as Palenque, Tikal, and Copan were abandoned. Invasion, overpopulation, and warfare have been proposed as possible causes, yet no single factor can completely explain the Classic Maya collapse.

Whatever its cause, the cities of the lowlands never recovered. The new rulers of the lowland cities were neither divine nor of the same Maya stock. During the post-Classic period (A.D. 1000–1521) the Petén Maya of Tabasco, along with the peoples of central Mexico, both unsettled and reshaped Maya civilization. The Maya of Yucatán became either conquered subjects or allies of the Toltecs. From their capital at Chichén Itzá they organized a trading empire that stretched from the Gulf Coast to Honduras. In the Highlands of Guatemala minor kingdoms were ruled by men who claimed descent from the Toltecs and their legendary leader, Quetzalcoatl, the Feathered Serpent.

The isolated centers in the Chiapas Highlands were able to maintain Classic traditions centuries after the collapse of cities along the Usumacinta River. In fact they probably prospered from the change, as Chiapas did not depend on other Maya centers for its wealth. Amber from the mines of Simojovel was traded throughout Mexico, and the plantations of Bochil were an important source of cacao beans that were accepted as currency by merchants everywhere. The great marketplace in Ixtapa, near the wells that supplied salt for the area, continued to thrive until the twelfth century; then waves of foreigners swept in. Maya from the Gulf Coast briefly controlled the region. In A.D. 1300 a group of fierce warriors called the Chiapanecs settled at a strategic point on the Grijalva River. For centuries they disrupted trade and battled with the Maya for possession of the salt wells and cacao plantations. Maya towns became walled fortresses warding off the Chiapanecs or Maya from rival communities. When the Spaniards arrived in the sixteenth century, the Maya joined with them in order to defeat their Chiapanec enemies.

Once the Spanish conquered the Chiapanecs—and named the province of Chiapas after them—they marched up to the Highlands and promptly enslaved the Maya. Chiapas history might have followed the same tragic path as the rest of Latin America had it not been for the intervention of the remarkable first bishop of Chiapas, Fray Bartolomé de Las Casas. He convinced King Philip II of Spain to free the Chiapas Maya, ban the conquistadores from Maya lands, and permit the Dominicans to convert the Maya peacefully to the True Faith. It was a noble experiment that succeeded in protecting the Chiapas Maya from some of the worst abuses of the conquest while convincing them to adopt the Catholic religion as their own. As time went on and the Church became more interested in tithes than in souls, the Maya periodically revolted, charging, with some justification, that the unchristian actions of the Church nullified its authority. Ironically, Chiapas Maya Catholicism retains the music, pageantry, and devotional rites introduced in the sixteenth century. Many of the rituals and beliefs that appear most exotic to observers are actually customs that were practiced four hundred years ago in Spain.

The Spanish Viceroyalty of Guatemala included all the states of Central America and Chiapas until 1825, when Chiapas joined the newly independent nation of Mexico. At that time the Pacific coast of Chiapas was a separate state known as the Soconusco, but it united with its neighbor when both became part of the new republic.

The state of Chiapas today includes a diversity of peoples and landscapes. Each region has its own identity, defined by its language and customs but most of all by its history. The invasions of non-Maya peoples—Chiapanecs, Aztecs, and Spaniards—along with the gods and philosophy they tried to impose are still the root of regional culture and conflicts.

The Soconusco was the home of many ancient peoples, including the Izapans, whose civilization dominated the Pacific coast between 500 B.C. and A.D. 100. A few years before the Spanish Conquest the So-

Mérida •

YUCATÁN

Chichén Itzá ▲

COZUMEL
ISLAND

CAPE
CATOCHE

QUINTANA
ROO

• Campeche

YUCATÁN
PENINSULA

Gulf of Mexico

CAMPECHE

M
É
X
I
C
O

• Chetumal

Hondo

▲ Cuello

TABASCO

Usumacinta

Caribbean Sea

Villahermosa •

PETÉN

Belize City

ERACRUZ

Palenque ▲

Piedras Negras ▲

Tikal ▲

BELIZE

San Andrés •
Chamula •

Tenejapa •

Yaxchilán ▲

Tuxtla Gutiérrez •

San Cristóbal
de Las Casas •

Bonampak ▲

OAXACA

Chiapa de Corzo •

LACANDON
JUNGLE

Zinacantan •

Grijalva

CHIAPAS

Lagartero •

GUATEMALA

SOCONUSCO COAST

▲ Copan

Izapa ▲

HONDURAS

▲ • Guatemala City

Kaminaljuyú

Tegucigalpa •

San Salvador •

EL SALVADOR

Pacific Ocean

• Cities and towns
▲ Archaeological sites

0   100

Statute Miles

NICARAGUA

conusco was an Aztec province, rich in cacao and cotton. Canals cut through the mangrove swamps were the main routes of trade and migration to Guatemala and beyond. Today the only rail line and the major highway to the south still run through the Soconusco. The sun-baked coast harbors simple villages where men fish for shrimp, sea bass, and shark. Vast cattle ranches and cotton plantations stretch across the dry, dusty plains.

Above the Soconusco rises the Sierra Madre, the "Mother of Mountains," the southern extension of the Rockies. Towering ceiba trees still shade cacao groves, and the chocolate of Chiapas remains a prized commodity. Now the slopes produce coffee. Maya from the Guatemalan and Chiapas Highlands seasonally migrate to the Soconusco to work on the giant coffee *fincas* (plantations), then return to their cold mountain homes.

On the other side of the Sierra Madre winds the Grijalva, a river as old as the mountains. The Grijalva River created a long, fertile valley between the Sierra Madre and the Highlands, then carved out of the mountains the Sumidero, one of the deepest canyons in the Americas.

The Grijalva formed a natural boundary between the Maya, who controlled the Highlands to the east, and the Zoques, who dominated the dry western half of Chiapas. The Zoques may be the descendants of the Olmecs, who invented the calendar the Maya later adopted. A stone with one of the earliest dates recorded, 54 B.C., was found at Chiapa de Corzo, a site on the Grijalva River right on the border between the Zoque and Maya territories.

The Grijalva River is now dammed above and below the Sumidero Canyon. Huge lakes fill the canyons behind the "Mothers of Electricity," as the Tzotzil Maya call the hydroelectric dams. Bananas, limes, and mangoes grow along the widening banks. When the Grijalva reaches the flat coastal plains, its brown waters move sluggishly past the cattle and oil fields of northern Chiapas and Tabasco, where it pours into the Gulf of Mexico.

The other great river of Chiapas, the Usumacinta, runs roughly parallel to the Grijalva and forms part of the border with Guatemala. The Usumacinta meanders through what was, until recently, a tropical rain forest called the Petén in Guatemala and the Lacandon in Chiapas.

The Lacandon jungle was populated by several different Maya groups. When the Spanish arrived, they brought new diseases that made the Lacandon forest almost uninhabitable. Soldiers and priests convinced the Chol and Tzeltal Maya who still lived there to abandon the jungle and move to the Highlands. One Chol tribe, however, rejected Christianity and fought off Spanish incursions until the end of the seventeenth century. They occupied a fortified island in Lake Miramar called Lakantun in Chol and Lacondon by Spanish chroniclers, who used the same term to describe the whole rain forest. During the colonial period a small group of Yucatec Maya fled into the rain forest to escape enslavement. They too renounced Christianity and returned to ancient customs. Since they lived as rebels in the Lacandon jungle, as their cousins did at Lakantun, they also became known as Lacandons. Today the Lacandon forest offers little refuge. Giant mahogany trees have been logged out. The recent discovery of oil has hastened the desecration of the jungle and its wildlife. Men who once hunted jaguars now drive trucks past the few magnificent trees left standing among grazing cattle and oil derricks.

The Highlands are more fortunate, in a sense, because there are few valuable resources to attract exploitation. In the center of the state, high above the shrinking forests and tropical scrub, the mountains appear inviolate. The poverty of the soil has kept the region a conservative bastion of Maya culture. Inadequate land has also forced Maya farmers to rent plots in the Grijalva Valley, pick coffee on the Soconusco

Zinacantec selling mineral salt in the San Cristóbal marketplace

fincas, or find jobs as construction workers in cities that mushroomed during the oil boom.

In the heart of the Highlands is the colonial city of San Cristóbal de Las Casas. San Cristóbal was settled almost a hundred years before the Pilgrims landed in Massachusetts. Spanish conquistadores built this provincial capital in 1524, after smashing the ancient Maya strongholds on the upper ridges.

San Cristóbal lies at the center of a jagged ring of mountains. Streams meander across the green valley, disappear into limestone caves, and flow forty miles underground to spill dark waters into the Grijalva River, a mile below. In the morning, fog hugs the valley floor. When the sun breaks through, the mist rises and the temperature climbs from near freezing to a sultry eighty degrees, plummeting again at twilight. Each afternoon during the rainy season the clouds pile up against the peaks at the western end of the valley until a boiling gray sky cracks and flashes with torrential rains. Suddenly the sky clears and the last rays of sun streak through the mountain gaps. A few stray clouds sink back into the ground. Lightning from distant storms silhouette the mountains, which frame the stars, moving close and forever.

For centuries San Cristóbal remained a backwater town whose only source of wealth was the taxation of the surrounding Maya population, which was savagely exploited and greatly feared. One English Dominican, Thomas Gage, who traveled through Chiapas in 1627, acknowledged the beauty of the towns but was less gracious about the inhabitants of San Cristóbal:

The city of Chiapa Real [San Cristóbal de Las Casas] is one of the meanest cities in all America, consisting of not above four hundred Spanish householders and about one hundred houses of Indians joining the city. . . . Here the merchants are close-handed and the gentlemen hard and sparing, wanting of wit and courtiers' parts and bravery. . . . Any small reason soon tires their weak brain, which is easily at stand when sense is propounded and slides on easily when nonsense carries the stream.

The people of San Cristóbal were not fools, but they were haunted by failed dreams of the wealth that the conquistadores had promised and the paradise on earth that the missionaries had hoped to bring about.

During the eighteenth and nineteenth centuries Maya communities staged rebellions against their oppressors, which, though brutally repelled, served to deepen the mistrust and hostility. As recently as fifteen years ago Maya in San Cristóbal were subject to strict restraints and denied equal rights by their Ladino (non-Indian Mexicans) neighbors. On the roads to the market, Ladino widows dressed in black preyed upon any Chamula or Tenejapan who carried a chicken or a heavy bag full of peanuts. Although a Maya man who touched a Ladino woman would be hunted down, these black widows had no fear of grabbing whatever goods they wanted and tossing the bearer a few pennies in exchange. The city lived off commerce with the Maya, yet any Indian found in town at night would be thrown into jail and forced to pay a fine. Despite the splendor of its churches and the talents and compassion of many of its inhabitants, San Cristóbal de Las Casas was, for the Maya, a cruel and petty place.

Relations between Ladinos and Maya are now much improved. The black widows have been banished from the marketplace, as San Cristóbal has finally grown out of its colonial past and become a commercial and governmental center that does not depend upon petty abuses to maintain its wealth and pride. With a fifth of the urban population now Maya, who have won control of half the market, San Cristóbal is no longer an isolated colony of Spaniards but a cosmopolitan center of all the peoples of the Highlands.

Leaving behind the past has created its own difficulties. In building a future, some of the quiet charm has been buried under concrete along with the less appealing aspects of the city. Walking down the street, loud with the sounds of traffic and radios, both Maya and Ladinos have arrived in the twentieth century, with all its problems and progress.

The roads of the Highlands all lead to San Cristóbal, which was my home as I traveled through Chiapas for over a decade, visiting each market and festival to collect textiles and study the designs. San Cristóbal is also a center for anthropological research, where I met many of the scholars whose collections of Maya oral literature reveal the beliefs of the people of Chiapas. I have humbly borrowed from their work for this book. Calixta Guiterez-Holmes's *Perils of the Soul* is a profound source of myths from Chenalhó. The autobiographies of women of Magdalenas, recorded by Amber Past in *Slo'il Jchi'iltaktik*, and the weavers' tales from Tenejapa translated by Francis Méndez are the best documentation of women's lives in Chiapas. Victoria Bricker's *Ritual Humor in the Highlands of Chiapas* relates many of the comic speeches given at the festivals of Zinacantan and Chamula. Gary Gossen's *Chamulas in the World of the Sun* is filled with delightful stories and anecdotes from Chamula. I have relied most heavily on Robert Laughlin's voluminous works on Zinacantan. Bob is a close friend who has given me access to his rich materials since I first arrived in Chiapas. The prayers, dreams, and myths from Zinacantan in this book are from Laughlin's *People of the Bat*.

The Quiché Maya epic of creation, *Popol Vuh*, written down in the sixteenth century, resounds in some of the modern stories recounted in Chiapas. Dennis Tedlock's fresh translation has breathed new life into this ancient work.

The Maya say that rainbows are the serpentine bones of the sky. Myths and dreams are the bones of this book.

The Maya in Time

Columbus never believed in the Americas: according to his calculations he was sailing through the Indies. He made four voyages to the Caribbean, absolutely certain that Asia and a lucrative trade in silk and spices lay just beyond the next island. On July 30, 1502, Columbus met a group of Maya sea traders on the Bay Islands off the coast of Honduras. The Maya clearly were more civilized than the "Indians" Columbus had seen before. For one thing, they wore clothes. Both men and women wore brilliantly colored capes that covered most of their bodies in a modest Christian fashion. The canoes in which they traveled were as long as Spanish galleys and had canopies over their centers to shade passengers and cargo. One canoe was piled high with textiles for trade, and another carried grains, fermented liquor, and money in the form of copper bells, hatchets, and cacao beans. Columbus had finally encountered a people with culture and wealth. It should have been a momentous day, but Columbus dismissed it. "The Navigator" was not interested in discovering the unknown; he knew where he was going.

The first Spaniards to land on Maya territory were lost. In 1511, the ship they were sailing from Panama to Santo Domingo struck a reef. Seventeen passengers and crew drifted in an open boat to the coast of Yucatán, where they were captured by Maya warriors. Some were sacrificed, others died of disease. Only two survived, Brother Gerónimo de Aguilar and Gonzalo Guerrero. The friar and the sailor came to radically different conclusions about the Maya. By the time the conquistadores arrived, Brother Gerónimo was praying for release from the heathen savages, and Gonzalo Guerrero was leading Maya warriors against his own people.

Six years after the castaways were washed ashore, the first Spanish military expedition, led by Fernando Hernandez, landed on Cape Catoche, at the tip of the Yucatán Peninsula. Maya canoes approached their boats, and with signs and gestures the natives invited the Spaniards to follow them to their city. When they marched into the plaza the Spaniards were ambushed by Maya archers, who killed seven men in the first volley. While the battle was raging, a Spanish priest rushed up the steps of the pyramid, ran into the temple, and grabbed the gold ornaments and statues that stood on the altar. The Spaniards were forced to retreat; it was Gonzalo Guerrero who directed the ambush that drove them off.

This first attempt to conquer the New World was a failure. Hernandez's ships barely made it back to Cuba. If it had not been for the quick reaction of the priest, the expedition would have had nothing to show for its troubles. The quality of the looted figurines impressed the governor of Cuba, who was certain they had been made by a civilized people. After examining the artifacts, he concluded that the Maya were descendants of the tribes of Jews that the Romans had expelled from Israel. Equally fascinating to the governor was the promise of finding more gold. He organized an expedition that was led by Juan de Grijalva with slightly more success in 1518 and another, in 1519, led by Hernán Cortéz.

Cortéz first landed on the island of Cozumel off the Yucatán coast. Cozumel had been a commercial and religious center for centuries. Maya seafarers traveling from the Gulf of Mexico to Honduras would stop at the island to trade goods and to visit the temple of the moon goddess Ix Chel, patroness of childbirth and weaving. Pilgrims from the mainland also flocked to this shrine, making Cozumel a lively marketing center.

The people of the island watched in dismay as Cortéz smashed the clay statues in the temple. The sanctuary atop the main pyramid was whitewashed and a cross built by the ship's carpenter placed in its center. Under Cortéz's command the Maya of Cozumel decorated the cross with fresh flowers. The Maya prayed that the new pilgrims would bring the peace and trade the conquistadores promised.

The goddess Ix Chel at her loom

From tales of previous expeditions Cortéz suspected that Spaniards were living among the natives on the mainland, and he directed the Maya lord of Cozumel to send messengers in search of them. Brother Gerónimo, after eight years of slavery, returned to his countrymen as soon as he was found. The story of his captivity and release was recorded by Bernal Díaz, one of Cortéz's soldiers who fought in each expedition to conquer Mexico and eventually was given the Chiapas Maya community of Chamula for his efforts.

Gerónimo de Aguilar remained a slave who labored in the cornfields of a Maya chief until the messenger from Cortéz arrived with a package of glass beads to pay for his release and a letter telling where the Spanish fleet lay at anchor. After attempting to convince Guerrero to come with him, Gerónimo used some of the beads to pay a crew of Maya to canoe him to the island of Cozumel. As soon as Gerónimo landed he climbed up the steps of the pyramid, stood before the cross, and preached to the Maya assembled in the plaza below the benefits of Christianity and the glories of the world to come.

Brother Gerónimo had little good to report about his compatriot Gonzalo Guerrero other than to mention that the Maya thought he was a brave man. According to Díaz's account, when the newly freed friar approached Guerrero to join up with Cortéz, Gonzalo Guerrero responded:

"Brother Aguilar, I am married and have three children, and they look on me as a cacique *[lord] here, and a captain in time of war. Go, and God's blessing be with you. But my face is tattooed and my ears are pierced. What would the Spaniards say if they saw me like this? And look how handsome these children of mine are! Please give me some of those beads you have brought, and I will tell them that my brothers have sent them from my own country." And Gonzalo's Indian wife spoke to Aguilar very angrily in her own language: "Why has this slave come here to call my husband away? Go off with you, and let us have no more talk."*

Then Aguilar spoke to Gonzalo again, reminding him that he was a Christian, and should not destroy his soul for the sake of an Indian woman. Besides, if he did not wish to desert his wife and children, he could take them with him. But neither words nor warnings could persuade Gonzalo to come.

When Gonzalo Guerrero was swept ashore he was probably enslaved along with the rest of the castaways. How he rose from captive to war captain and the husband of the local lord's daughter is not recorded, but he must have been a remarkable man.

Guerrero, not convinced that Christianity was the path to salvation, continued to attack the conquistadores. Perhaps it was a futile cause, but the cities of the Yucatán continued to repulse Spanish incursions a generation after the Aztec empire had collapsed. In the region where Guerrero lived, in what is now the state of Quintana Roo, the Maya of the hinterlands did not submit to foreign rule until the Mexican army marched into their last stronghold in 1900.

Guerrero and Brother Gerónimo, the first Spaniards to live among the Maya, held opposing views about the essential nature of the people of the New World, whether they were human or animal. The debate continued to fester as the conquistadores marched on. The first bishop of Chiapas, Fray Bartolomé de Las Casas, enraged the veterans of the

Dominican friars preaching in Chiapas

conquest by declaring that Indians had souls and therefore some minimal human rights. When he freed the Maya slaves and excommunicated the entire Spanish population of Chiapas for unchristian behavior, threats on his life forced him to flee. Questions about the morality of Spanish rule are rarely raised in accounts of the conquistadores, who had few doubts that they were fighting the good fight for God and King and whatever spoils came their way.

This unwavering faith in the righteousness of their cause permeates Bernal Díaz's chronicle, along with the awe and fear the soldiers felt as they fought their way through alien country. Díaz describes seeing the Aztec capital of Tenochitlán for the first time:

These great towns . . . and buildings rising from the water, all made of stone, seemed like an enchanted vision. . . . Indeed, some of our soldiers asked whether it was not all a dream. . . . It was all so wonderful that I do not know how to describe this first glimpse of things never heard of, seen or dreamed of before. . . . [The palaces] were very spacious and well built, of magnificent stone, cedar wood, and the wood of other sweet-smelling trees, with great rooms and courts, which were a wonderful sight, and all covered with awnings of woven cloth. . . . But today all that I then saw is overthrown and destroyed. Nothing is left standing.

After the fall of Tenochitlán, Díaz moved on to the conquest of Chiapas.

The peoples of Chiapas had been warring for centuries. In the Highlands, Chamulas and Zinacantecs struggled over control of land trade routes. They were unified only in their common hatred for the Chiapanecs, who dominated trade along the Grijalva River. When the Spanish arrived from the west, accompanied by Aztec troops, the Maya recognized them as potential allies.

The Spaniards were repulsed by the Chiapanecs in their first encounter, although as Díaz reports the priestess who led the Chiapanecs into battle was slain:

They brought into the middle of their troops an Indian woman, somewhat old and fat, saying that since she had joined the fighting we would be conquered. She carried an incense burner and some stone idols. Her whole body was painted, with cotton stuck to the paint. Fearless she went among the Indians who were our allies, and that damned goddess was chopped to bits!

Chiapanec slaves revolted and gave the Spaniards dugout canoes to enable them to cross the Grijalva and take the magnificent city of Chiapa. The Spanish conquistadores conquered a great metropolis:

We entered the city in formation and when we came to the most populated area, where stood their great pyramids and temples, the houses were so close together that we could not pitch camp and had to do so out in the fields.

The Zinacantecs were delighted to hear of the defeat of their old enemies and sent representatives to swear allegiance to the Spaniards. The Chamulas at first accepted Spanish rule and joined in their fight against the Chiapanecs, but when a lone soldier went to them demanding gold, they revolted. The Spanish captain, Luis Marin, was outraged by the soldier's action and ordered him to walk back

Captain Luis Marin

to Mexico City and report to Cortéz. According to Díaz, Marin asked the Chamulas to surrender, but they refused. The Spaniards immediately employed two hundred Zinacantec bearers and marched on Chamula.

Meanwhile, the Chamulas had retreated to a citadel high atop sheer limestone cliffs. Warriors pelted the Spaniards with "so many stones, sticks, and arrows that they covered the ground." There was no way to enter the stronghold by direct assault. A thousand Chamula warriors armed with obsidian-tipped lances defended the battlements. Storming the walls was impossible because the fall was so great that the soldiers would be smashed to pieces. As Díaz says, "It was not something to try."

Instead, the Spaniards used the same device that Caesar had used to defeat the Gauls. The soldiers constructed an elevated platform large enough to cover twenty men and moved it next to the walls to protect the troops while they dug a hole under the fortification. The Chamulas threw down rotten fish and boiling oil, pots of boiling water mixed with blood, and rocks large enough to smash the platform. But it was soon repaired, and the soldiers continued to work. According to Díaz:

When they saw that we were making larger holes, four priests came out on their battlements covered with cloth or wooden shields and said, "Well, if what you want and desire is gold, come inside, we have plenty," and they threw down seven diadems of fine gold, many hollow beads and other beads made in the form of shells and ducks, all made of gold. And after that came many arrows, sticks and stones. . . . The Chamulas played drums and blew trumpets all night, shouting and screaming that they would kill us, for that is what their idol promised.

The Spanish attack against Chamula

Their gifts did not appease the Spaniards, however, who kept digging beneath the fortification until the walls were breached. The Chamulas fought bravely to repel the invaders, as Díaz testifies:

Suddenly we entered through one of the holes, myself and a companion, and there were two hundred warriors piled on top of us thrusting their lances. If it was not for the quick assistance of the Zinacantecan Indians we would have lost our lives.

The Chiapas Highlands became a Spanish province under the rule of God and King. As Cortéz had promised, Bernal Díaz was given a special reward for his service as a soldier—all the land and tribute of Chamula. The conquistadores expected a rich booty from a people who possessed golden diadems, but the Chamulas did not care for gold, and what little they owned had already been thrown in disgust at the Spaniards. When the troops entered Chamula, they grabbed the women and children and the few men who remained, but they could not find any treasures to loot.

The Spanish troops led their prisoners down to the valley and set up camp beside a stream. The first Spanish mayor of the rude camp called it Villa Viciosa, "Village of Vice," because the main source of commerce was selling captured Maya as slaves. This settlement, which became the capital of the province of Chiapas, is now known as San Cristóbal de Las Casas.

The destruction of Maya cities, the enslavement of the people, and the imposition of a new religion should have been enough to destroy Maya culture. The Maya were reduced to peasantry, their books burned, and their nobility impoverished through taxation. Painting, sculpture, and other fine arts were banned as idolatrous.

The Maya chiefs attempted to preserve their prerogatives by adopting the appearance of the foreign culture. When Bartolomé de Las Casas arrived in San Cristóbal in 1545, he found the young Maya nobles dressed in the style of the Spanish conquistadores. They soon discovered that they had been given over to new lords who wore a different cloth.

Bishop Las Casas brought with him a decree from

Church and convent of Santo Domingo

King Philip II that placed all Maya communities of the Highlands under the sole jurisdiction of the Dominican order. Bernal Díaz and his fellow conquistadores were stripped of their titles to Maya lands. The Dominicans under Bishop Las Casas pledged to convert the Maya to Christianity, preach to the converts in their own language, administer to their needs, and protect them from the depravations of civil authorities. The Kingdom of God was at hand.

Bishop Las Casas's father had sailed with Columbus, and Las Casas himself had been a soldier and a landowner before he was called by God and entered the Dominican order. Las Casas, as did many converts, became a most ardent Christian and a passionate defender of the oppressed. His relentless attacks on the conquistadores for their harsh treatment of the Indians placed him in certain jeopardy, and he was forced to flee to Spain. His Dominican brethren established their first monastery in Zinacantan, close to San Cristóbal. From there they began the conversion of the Highland Maya and, from a distance, monitored their Spanish flock.

The first friars who established the monastery landed in Campeche. From there they struggled on the road from Palenque through the mountains. The trip took two months. Fray Tomás de la Torre describes the trip:

Fray Tomás de San Juan was very sick during the travels and thus it was agreed to send him ahead in a hammock. . . . It is a pleasant thing to travel that way, although some become seasick. These people use them to carry their lords and principal persons and the sick and it is in them that the women of Castile travel on trips and even the Spanish men are themselves carried in them when they go to their towns, especially when the road is bad and they cannot go on horseback.

The early friars took up their mission with great zeal, and the Maya, grateful for their protection, converted wholeheartedly to Christianity. The friars taught that the essential elements of the faith involved devotion to the saints, which included public rituals, music, and processions in their honor. The Maya never forgot those teachings; the Dominicans soon lost sight of their goal of creating a peaceful kingdom on earth.

Within a decade of Bishop Las Casas's arrival, the Domincans began to accommodate the local authorities and accepted their offer of the labor of twenty thousand Maya to build a more comfortable convent and church in San Cristóbal. The result, the Church of Santo Domingo, is a Baroque masterpiece of gold leaf and stone. Surrounding the images of pale saints and cherubim, gilded plants and vines twist and curl under the new light of Christianity. The double-headed eagle, symbol of the Hapsburg Empire (of which Spain was the crown), perches above the western door.

By the end of the sixteenth century Dominican friars, sitting in the grand monasteries built with Maya labor and surrounded by European design and art, felt confident that the old traditions had been replaced by a new, Christian order. The Maya people, however, saw no reason to forget their ancestors.

The Maya had built and abandoned many great cities long before the arrival of the Spaniards. Those cities had no gold, however, and so held little interest for the soldiers and priests who were searching for treasure. Three centuries after the Spanish Conquest, European and American explorers discovered the monumental ruins of Palenque, Copan, and Tikal draped with a thousand years of tropical growth. Certain that they had found a lost civilization, these explorers thought it preposterous that the impoverished peasants who lived near the ruins could have had anything to do with the building of what was obviously a great culture. And so they invented an extinct race of "Noble Maya," descendants of an advanced civilization from another continent.

Speculations on the mysterious sculptures of men and gods surrounded by indecipherable hieroglyphic texts led to sensational stories of Atlantis and the Lost Tribes of Israel. Scholarship apparently had advanced very little since the sixteenth century, when the governor of Cuba declared the first piece of Maya sculpture brought back from Mexico to be the work of Jews. Other experts thought the Maya temples had been built by Egyptians, Greeks, Vikings, Phoenicians—anyone except the Maya living in the area. One nineteenth-century English scholar, Viscount Kingsborough, spent his life and entire fortune trying to prove that the hieroglyphic texts were Hebrew. On the other hand, P. T. Barnum made a fortune by presenting to Queen Victoria's court a pair of microcephalic dwarfs he claimed were the last degenerate

Frederick Catherwood's drawing of the Palenque frieze of the Lord of the Underworld, which appeared in John Lloyd Stephens's book Incidents of Travel in Central America, Chiapas and Yucatan

remains of a caste of high priests, found, at great expense, in a lost Maya city.

The explorers of the nineteenth century were looking for a lost civilization, and, supported by elaborate theories and far-fetched "proofs," they projected their favorite philosophy onto the exotic ruins. Consequently, many of the important discoveries about the Maya have been made not by scholars but by amateurs with few preconceptions and little training in the field.

The clearest descriptions of Maya ruins were written by John Lloyd Stephens. An American lawyer sent to Central America in 1839 to negotiate a proposed canal through Nicaragua, Stephens discovered that the area was in the midst of a civil war, and he could not find a government with which he could negotiate. To occupy his time he visited Maya ruins in Central America and Mexico. Fredrick Catherwood, an artist who accompanied him, made careful drawings of the monuments and buildings, and together they produced two travel books that became immediate best-sellers. Stephens proposed several theories about the Maya, among them that Maya sculptures were portraits of ancient rulers and that the Maya of today are the descendants of those rulers. His ideas later proved to be true, although they were ignored by the scholars of his day.

At the end of the nineteenth century a librarian in Dresden, Ernst Forstemann, deciphered the Maya calendar. He kept a rare Maya codex in the top drawer of his desk for twenty years so that he could look at the strange screenfold book in his free moments. Many of the glyphs in the text remained a mystery to him, but he eventually deduced that the mathematical calculations, written in bars and dots, described planetary cycles. Forstemann then studied how the Maya counted time. Maya calendrics is very complicated. The Maya had two intermeshing "years" of 260 and 365 days. These were tied to a "Long Count," which tallied the total number of days that had elapsed since August 13, 3114 B.C., the beginning of the Maya world. Forstemann's decipherment allowed scholars to read the calendrical inscriptions found on the monuments.

This discovery naturally caused a great deal of excitement, even though dates alone did not explain the meaning behind the monuments. During the first half of the twentieth century, archaeologists excavated a number of new sites in the jungle, and researchers scoured libraries for colonial documents on the Maya. Despite the growing mass of data, the hieroglyphs remained largely indecipherable. Since the majority of the hieroglyphs on the monuments were dates and calculations, scholars concluded that the Maya were obsessed with time. They were seen as a peaceful people who spent their days observing the stars and carving stelae with portraits of anonymous astronomer-priests to commemorate important celestial phenomena.

Modern research, particularly the recent decipherment of the hieroglyphs, has dispelled these romantic notions of Maya civilization. Stephens was right; Maya monuments do portray historical rulers, and the dates on the stelae celebrate their birth, accession to the throne, and glorious victories in battle. Classic Maya kings were military leaders and self-proclaimed gods who sacrificed rival kings in brutal ritual wars. They were also poets, priests, and patrons of the arts. Maya painting, sculpture, architecture, and literature flourished under divine rule.

Now that scholars can read the hieroglyphs, we know the names of Classic Maya kings and can begin to understand Maya history from the Maya point of view. We know, for example, that Pacal the Great transformed Palenque from a small village into a major Maya city during the seventh century. *Pacal* means "shield" and can be written as a single pictograph of a shield or as a hieroglyph composed of three phonetic signs that represent the syllables *pa-ka-la*, with the final vowel silent. The "alphabet" used by Maya scribes was extremely creative. The sound *ta* could be written as a cursive sign or as a

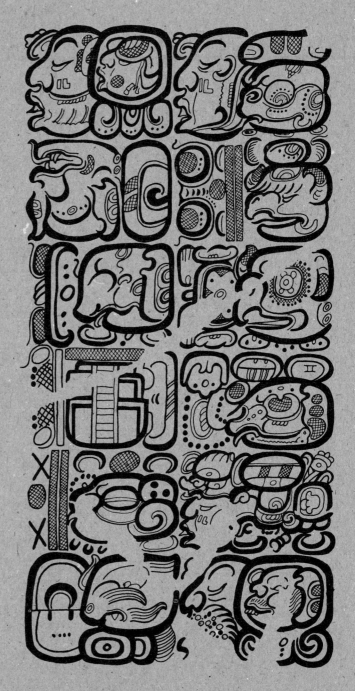

The opening lines from an eighth-century panel of inscriptions from Palenque. Pacal the Great is referred to twice in these lines: on the third row on the right, the bird's eye is the pictograph for shield, which means "pacal," and the glyph that follows shows the front staircase of the pyramid where Pacal was buried

Two nobles from Bonampak, A.D. 791

pictograph of the head of a vulture called *tahol*. Scribes strove to invent new combinations of images and sounds to express the nuances of the language.

Maya nobles were accomplished in the arts. The life they led in their palace courts was rich and sophisticated. The eighth-century murals of Bonampak show that their clothing, hardly a necessity in the tropics, was extremely elaborate. The divine kings wore painted and brocaded hipcloths, capes, and turbans, along with back-frames of quetzal feathers that formed an iridescent blue-green aura around them. Royal musicians and dancers wore jade ear plugs, heavy jade necklaces, and enormous headdresses decorated with carved masks, fish, feathers, and lotus blossoms.

The costumes depicted in Maya art help explain the action of the scene, its ceremonial and metaphysical significance. Since public monuments were intended for viewing by a semiliterate population, the texts are brief. They state the name of the nobles

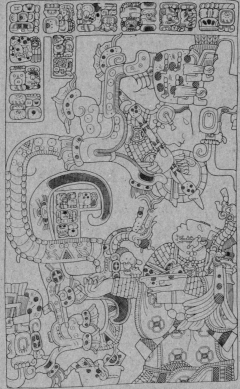

Yaxchilán Lintel 24

Yaxchilán Lintel 25

Yaxchilán Lintel 26

portrayed, the ritual event depicted, and the date it was performed, much as footnotes to the complex scenes carved in stone. The ritual implements and the costumes worn are the real "text" that the average Maya could read without difficulty.

At Yaxchilán, a huge Maya site on the Usumacinta River, three lintels over the portals of one of the temples show scenes of a bloodletting ritual. The hieroglyphs state that Lady Xoc and her husband, Shield Jaguar, performed this sacrificial rite on the anniversary of his accession to the throne of Yaxchilán. In the first scene, on Lintel 24, Lady Xoc is seen kneeling before Shield Jaguar and passing a rope of thorns through her tongue. Bloodstained paper lies in a basket at her feet. Lady Xoc wears a rectangular gown, or *huipil*, that is brocaded with diamond-

bound with woven signs for the sky and planets. Wearing this ceremonial robe, Lady Xoc symbolically stands at the crossroads, at the center of the world, where she can communicate with her divine ancestors.

The act of bloodletting induces hallucinations, and Lady Xoc is prepared for the vision she will receive. Shield Jaguar has already offered his blood. The tip of his staff has burst into flame.

In the next lintel, smoke rising from the offering of bloodstained paper is transformed into snakes. A double-headed serpent coils above Lady Xoc, and from its maw emerges a warrior wearing a jaguar-skin helmet. Unafraid, Lady Xoc displays her offerings to the royal supernatural. The design on her garment is a four-petaled flower that symbolizes the

shaped designs representing the four quarters of the world moving through time. The edge of the *huipil* is

mouth of Cauac, the reptilian earth monster whose jaws receive and disgorge dead souls. This design is cut out of the cloth to form an opening, like the mouth it represents, and in the center is a braided knot, the glyph for royalty. Lady Xoc wears what she sees—a royal personage emerging from the jaws of the underworld.

The warrior who appeared in Lady Xoc's vision is played by her husband in the final scene. Shield Jaguar is dressed for battle in cotton armor studded with stone disks. Flint knife in hand, he receives his flexible shield and jaguar helmet from his wife. She wears a *huipil* similar to that worn in the first scene, but instead of a symbol of the earth, there is an image of a toad at the center of the diamonds. The toad is

commonly associated with the beginning of the rainy season, when the newly planted cornfields are filled with toads singing and mating in the first spring showers. The toad symbolizes the rains that bring life and fertility to the earth. Its curled legs resemble the pictograph for accession: the crossed legs of the king seated on the stone platform that serves as his throne. The toad motif is worn by the queen as an emblem of prosperity under Shield Jaguar's reign.

His reign, though prosperous, was not peaceful. After this ritual Shield Jaguar led his war captains in an attack on a neighboring kingdom for loot, slaves, and sacrificial victims. Shield Jaguar emphasized his military prowess on public monuments in order to maintain control over his own nobles and those of nearby sites, such as Bonampak. His wives (at least three are named in the inscriptions) represented his political alliances with these powerful chiefs, known as *cahals*.

The divine kings and queens of the Classic Maya were more than political and military leaders: they were the emissaries between this world and the next, where the Ancestors and gods directed the renewal

of life. The tomb of Pacal at Palenque, deep within the pyramid and buried under tons of stone and rubble, was connected by a small air passage to the top of the temple so that Pacal could still be addressed by his descendants. His sarcophagus is flanked by portraits of his ancestors and sealed with a massive stone slab that depicts his descent through the open maw of the earth monster into the underworld.

The Lords of Xibalba, the lords of death and disease, would be the first to greet the dead ruler and put him through a series of trials. As described in the *Popol Vuh*, he would have to pass a different test each night and play a ball game with the lords of death each day. As did the Hero Twins of the myth, the king expected to emerge victorious from death's domain, to live not on the surface of the earth again but among his ancestors in the underworld.

The Maya underworld is difficult to place. *Yut Balumil*—"Inside the Earth"—is one of the names a Tzotzil Maya shaman uses to describe the underworld. *Ch'ul Vinajel*—"Holy Heaven"—is the term used to describe the mountaintop shrines where he or she goes to speak directly to the Ancestors, just as the people of Palenque climbed the pyramid to address their dead lord, Pacal. In Classic Maya art the underworld is portrayed as a subterranean palace, a land surrounded by aquatic life under a blood-red sea, or beyond the stars and planets on a path through the Milky Way.

The Hero Twins, after defeating the lords of death, rose into the heavens, where one brother became the sun and the other Venus. The first appearance of Venus as the evening star on the horizon was the time of ritual war fought between kings, who reenacted the heroic adventures of the gods. Myths and history were ordained by the movements of the stars.

Maya astronomers plotted the orderly motion of the heavens, the seasons, years, and days. They fixed the beginning of the present creation on a day some three thousand years before the first Classic Maya monument was erected. Yet the Maya believed in even earlier creations and probably conceived of a universe with no beginning or end. The hieroglyphic inscriptions record deities performing rituals thousands of years in the future and billions of years in the past.

The world ended and renewed itself in progressive cycles, day by day, year by year, in epochs defined by planetary conjunctions or sacred numbers. The end of one such epoch occurred during the ninth century. At Lagartero, Chiapas, hundreds of figurines, painted bowls, and plates were made as part of an elaborate end-of-cycle ceremony. The earth was opened for the ritual and a man sacrificed and buried in the pit, along with a dog to carry his soul to the underworld. At the end of the ceremony the figurines, along with every piece of pottery in the city, were smashed and buried to clear the way for a new epoch. That epoch never arrived. After this Lagartero was used only as a graveyard. For all we know the artists who made the figurines, and all the men and women they had portrayed, quietly abandoned the city.

By A.D. 900 the cities of Palenque, Yaxchilán, Copan, and Tikal had fallen. Famine, war, or social unrest, in some combination, may have been contributory factors; no one calamity can fully explain why the lowland cities decayed. Current theories about the collapse of Classic Maya civilization mirror our concerns and fears about the possible sudden failure of our own culture. What is often forgotten is that although the Classic cities toppled, new cities rose up and new rulers came to power. The Classic Maya collapse did not mean an end to Maya culture but an end to the rule of divine kings. The post-Classic center of Chichén Itzá may lack a certain subtlety and grace, yet it organized a powerful empire based on commerce and cultural exchange. One thing is certain: the Maya never disappeared. They continued to record their histories, prophecies, and astronomical calculations in hieroglyphic codices until the last Maya city in Guatemala fell to the Spanish at the end of the seventeenth century.

Ceramic figurine of a Maya lord from Lagartero

Maya hieroglyphic writing was banned as demonic by the Spanish missionaries in an attempt to erase the native culture, although the friars learned Maya to preach to their new converts; these same friars also trained Maya nobles to write their languages phonetically using the Roman alphabet. Books were secretly written by the Maya to record the knowledge of their ancestors, a few of which survived the Inquisitions of the colonial period, including the most important—the *Popol Vuh*, an ancient hieroglyphic codex transliterated into Quiché Maya verse.

Stories in the *Popol Vuh* about the gods of the underworld and their defeat by the Hero Twins are depicted in the earliest Maya art and are still recounted in myths and legends familiar to all Maya. The exploits of the Quiché Hero Twins of Guatemala, Hunahpu and Ixbalanque, are attributed in Chenalhó, Chiapas, to Kox—"little brother Christ"—but the plots and morals are the same.

Many of the ceremonies practiced in the Highlands today are of Pre-Columbian origin. In the annual ceremonial exchange of authority from one religious leader to another, the procession of the new official up the ladder to a wooden platform made holy through sacrifice was once part of the Classic Maya ritual of a king's ascension to the throne.

Likewise, time is still regulated by the ancient calendar, with its eighteen months of twenty days and five "lost days" at the end of the year when "the world turned upside down." Ceremonial garments are woven with designs that, for millennia, have depicted the Maya cosmos and the supernatural beings that

Weaving design of the Holy Toad, from San Andrés

make the world flower. Living Maya culture has preserved much of the ancient traditions at the deepest layer of belief. Influences from the Aztecs, the Spaniards, and modern technocrats have been absorbed into a profound and complex culture.

The Maya of the Highlands continue to live in communities that were formed long before the conquest. They were allowed to remain in the Highlands because the area was too cold to produce tropical crops for export. The most valuable areas of the lowlands were seized by the Spanish, and what was left over was taken by non-Indian Mexicans after the Mexican Independence. Dominican friars established huge plantations of sugarcane in the Grijalva Valley that are still in operation under new owners. Cotton, which was plentiful in the lowlands, was another important export crop, as was the dye from indigo plants. Cochineal, an insect that feeds on the nopal cactus and produces a permanent red stain, was worth its weight in gold.

As tribute to the Spanish, Maya were forced to labor on the cacao plantations of the Soconusco coast, where they rarely survived the tropical diseases that the conquistadores and their African slaves had brought to the New World. The Maya, like Indians throughout the Spanish colonies, were often worked to death building churches and *haciendas* for their new lords. When Mexico broke loose from Spain in the nineteenth century, the situation grew even worse. New laws set up a system known as debt peonage. The Maya call this the time of slavery, for once a man was indebted to a rancher, lumber company, or coffee plantation it was almost impossible to work off what he owed. His sons would inherit his debts and they too would be forced into indenture for the rest of their lives. This caused a shortage of men in the Highlands; by the end of the nineteenth century over half the households in Zinacantan were headed by women. The Mexican Revolution in 1910 swept away these laws and eventually returned some of the land that had been stolen during the time of slavery. The Maya who had been debt peons for over a generation were freed by revolutionary troops and sent home.

The Maya did not accept these abuses passively but revolted numerous times against their masters. What rankled them most was the corruption and taxation of the Church that had promised them heaven and finally left them in hell. The Maya remain faithful to the teachings of the first friars and consider themselves true Christians—*Batz'i Kristiano*—as opposed to the Ladinos, also called *Kaxlan* (Castilians).

The Earthlord, a design from San Andrés

Kaxlan is also a name of the Earthlord, the being who lives in the mountains controlling the riches of the earth. It is somehow appropriate that one of the few totally non-Catholic figures of Chiapas Maya religion is described as a fat Ladino who buys and sells souls.

Many of the Catholic rituals taught to the Maya were already familiar to them, to the great surprise of the early missionaries. The Maya practiced baptism in water, confirmation, fasting, and sexual abstinence before rituals. They incensed and dressed their idols just as the friars would later ask them to do for the statues of the saints. The cross was a familiar icon, used in Maya hieroglyphs that refer to celestial bodies and appearing in the form of the World Tree on the tomb of Pacal in Palenque. When the friars explained that the cross was the sign of God, who had died on the Tree of Good and Evil and now lives in the heavens, the Maya accepted it as another version of a story they already knew.

The mythology of the Maya of Chiapas joins Catholic and old Maya beliefs into a new vision of the sacred nature of the world. Jesus, Mary, and the saints have become the central characters in stories based on the Bible as well as the *Popol Vuh*. Their religion is essentially Christian, translated into Maya using the signs and metaphors of the sacred that are an integral part of Maya language and culture.

The Maya blend history and myth. They place events not in the order of their occurrence but in order of their importance. The leader of land reform in 1938, Erasto Urbina, appears in Chamula stories about "the beginning of the world." Some storytellers are old enough to remember the actions that Erasto undertook to restore Chamula land and basic rights, yet Erasto is an actor in ancient myth because he changed the world of Chamula and caused its renewal.

Historical events are part of the underlying reality of the present. The nature of daily existence and the value of traditional approaches to the world are validated through tales of the past. The characters in Maya myths are generally average people who behave correctly in extraordinary circumstances. On the other hand, supernatural beings in Maya myths are more human than godlike and frequently appear in the mundane world. For example, the story of the building of the church of Salinas in Zinacantan begins:

Long ago, when Salinas was formed, the Virgin appeared to a young boy.

"What are you doing, son?" asked the Virgin.

The Hearthstones, one of the sacred mountains of Zinacantan

"I'm taking a walk around my little cornfield, ma'am. I'd like to clear the brush, since the planting season has arrived."

"So that's what you're doing! I am very pleased by this holy place. I'd like to be seated here. I'd like you to build a little house for me."

The truths revealed in myths animate the landscape. Each place, each community is special because it has been touched by God. And each community sees the hand of God as if it moves for its people alone.

The people of San Andrés Larráinzar tell a story of how their patron saint, Saint Andrew, banished the ocean to provide his people with a place to live. The Highlands of Chiapas were indeed once a seabed. The limestone of the ancient ocean floor appears as white streaks across the mountains. Seashells and fossils of sea creatures are visible in boulders that slowly erode in millennial rains.

According to the legend, Saint Andrew defeated a monster called Hairy Hand, who controlled the waters, and sent him over the mountains to create the Caribbean Sea. Saint Andrew was gracious in victory and invited Hairy Hand to come back and visit, especially on the saint's feast day in November. And sure enough, after the people have swept the market square, hired the musicians, prepared the ritual meals, and built castles of fireworks in honor of their patron saint, the clouds roll in and a substantial proportion of the Caribbean drops on San Andrés.

In contrast, the Maya of Chamula, neighboring San Andrés, believe that a properly conducted festival will always occur under sunny skies. It is not coincidence that their main festival, Carnaval, falls in the middle of the dry season and the festival of their patron saint in a short dry period in June.

In January the rains slow down, in March and April the skies are cloudless, and by May the fields of last year's corn stalks are brown, bent-over skeletons among the weeds. Then the farmers crop the stubble and burn the fields, releasing clouds of smoke and soot that blot out the hills and sun in imitation of the rainy season that is about to begin. Plants grow by the inch in the first rains of May, when the soot is washed from the sky. From June to September it rains most afternoons, except for a few weeks around the solstice. The rains pause just as the sun stops moving north, and they return in full force when the sun's path begins to angle southward. In this sunny interval the Chamulas hold a festival in honor of their patron saint, Saint John. During the fall and sporadically in the winter the tails of Pacific and Caribbean hurricanes whip across the Highlands, bringing torrential rains and cold fog that last for days. These storms are called *k'in nebal*, the "festival of clouds."

It is difficult to hold a human festival when the clouds are celebrating at the same time, so the Chamula officials who are responsible for the festival of Carnaval take precautions. The men, called *Pasiónes*, must fast, pray, and abstain from sleeping with their wives for forty days before the festival. Thousands of Chamulas come to the center to watch the *Pasiónes* pray, dance, and parade around the central square, then run through fire in a final act of purification. If it rains during Carnaval, the elders meet to decide which *Pasión* irked God by being too passionate with his wife. The offending *Pasión* is jailed until the rains let up.

When Chamulas hear about the rained-out festivals of San Andrés they laugh and conjecture about the amorous affairs of the religious leaders who brought on the disaster. Although the people of San Andrés must quietly question the wisdom of their patron saint's invitation to Hairy Hand, no one in San Andrés is ever jailed for rain. Each of the fifty Maya communities in the Highlands has a slightly different idea of how the universe works.

Continuing debates among communities concerning the truth of their myths keep traditions lively and creative. Although each community generally thinks of itself as independent and superior to the rest, myths reveal how important neighbors are to the world they share.

A tale about Venus and the sun, as told by Tonik Nibak of Zinacantan, describes how the townsfolk first rejected, then accepted, the possibility that a neighbor may play an important role in the universe.

The great star appeared. The sky grew bright from end to end.

"I am the sweeper of the path. I sweep Our Lord's path so that when Our Lord passes by he finds the path already swept."

Venus is the morning star. She is a girl from Chamula.

The women didn't believe the Chamulan girl who said she was a star.

"She says she is a star! Could she be a star? She's an awful, ugly, black Chamulan. Isn't the star a beautiful bright red?" said the women.

"I am the one who fixes the path. When Our Lord disappears, the ocean dries up. The fish come out of the sea. When Our Lord disappears, there is a red sun, the monkey's sun.

"I am the sweeper of the house. I walk when it grows light. When night falls, I sweep beneath the world. When dawn comes, I appear and sweep again, because that is my work. That's why I am a star. Venus appears early in the dawn, say the people, but it's me. I sweep Our Lord's path. It isn't just anyone's path."

She sweeps the path off constantly. When she disappears, she is traveling inside the earth. When the star reappears the next morning, she sweeps the path again, the path of the holy sun.

We didn't believe that it was a Chamulan girl. "It seems to be a star, but a Chamulan, I don't believe it!" we said.

But the poor girl heard us mocking her. If it weren't so, she wouldn't have heard. But she did hear, so it's true.

Every act, even one as humble as sweeping, is given dignity and importance in the world described through myths. Today's daily chores—making a tortilla, cutting wood, weaving—are the same chores performed by heroes and gods at the beginning of time, acts that began the world and that keep it alive.

The Highlands

Built as a portal to the underworld in the eighth century, Palenque stands in the foothills of the Chiapas Highlands, facing the setting sun. Maya kings were believed to have the power to defeat the Lords of Death and return in dreams and visions to advise the living. The Maya abandoned their stone cities many centuries ago, but they remained on their land and still listen to their ancestors in dreams.

One million Maya live in the Chiapas Highlands today. Each mountain and valley has a different climate: some are temperate zones, where apples and oranges grow side by side; others are tropical or bitten by winter frosts. Maya communities are equally diverse. Neighboring communities may speak different Maya languages, and each has its own style of ritual and costume. This diversity does not fragment the culture, but keeps it alive: the constant and subtle debate between communities as to which interpretation of a common tradition is most valid confirms their striving to define the proper way of life and preserves the basic belief in the wisdom of the Ancestors.

Maya kings of the Classic period (A.D. 100–900) were thought to be divine; their palaces were built to shield them from the common people. The enclosed courtyards of the royal palace in Palenque (preceding page) were used for private theaters and ceremonies, including the offering of royal blood to the gods, the rulers' direct ancestors. Maya kings offered their own blood and went to war to capture rulers of neighboring communities for sacrifice.

In the observatory tower in the center of the Palenque palace small portals were aligned to enable the sighting of Venus's first appearance on the horizon, the signal to begin warfare. If the king and his warriors were successful, their captives would be brought back to carve a monument attesting to the rule of the king (such as the stones from Palenque above) before being sacrificed.

After nearly a millennium of rule by divine kings Classic Maya civilization collapsed in the tenth century. The cities were abandoned and the portraits of the kings defaced. The Maya did not disappear, however, and neither did their culture. In Yucatán the Maya joined with Toltec people from central Mexico to form an empire that stretched from the Gulf Coast to Honduras. Their largest city was Chichén Itzá, built alongside Classic Maya ruins sometime after A.D. 1000; its buildings, such as the *Castillo* (opposite) reflect the severe lines of Toltec architecture. By 1300 this empire too broke apart, but the Maya continued to keep astronomical records and preserve their history and culture in hieroglyphic books.

ABOVE: The Chiapas Highlands rise 9,000 feet above the sea. Surrounded by tropical lowlands and rain forests, the pine- and oak-forested mountains stand coolly isolated from the rest of the state. In the summer the damp ocean air condenses around the mountain peaks, and in the fall the tails of hurricanes from the Pacific Ocean and the Gulf of Mexico whip across the Highlands, dropping torrential rains. Clouds cling to the highest ridges throughout the year, forming pockets of moist, cool jungle in which spider monkeys, jaguarundis, and lemurs live among the bamboo and orchids that grow in the mist.

OPPOSITE: During the colonial period following the Spanish Conquest, Spaniards expropriated the verdant lowlands for plantations of sugar cane and other tropical crops that could be exported to Spain. The Maya in the Highlands kept their land, but most men must come down from the mountains to work part of each year as day laborers in construction work or to farm parcels of lowland fields rented from Mexican ranchers.

The people of the Lacandon jungle, in the eastern part of Chiapas bordering Guatemala, refused to be conquered or converted to Christianity. When the last Maya strongholds were defeated at the end of the seventeenth century, refugees fled to the Lacandon and formed small settlements dispersed throughout the jungle. Dubbed Lacandons by rubber-tree tappers who ventured into the jungle in the 1800s, the people still make pilgrimages to the ruins at Palenque and Yaxchilán, considered to be the home of the gods, and Lacandon men continue to wear their hair long and dress in the simple style of their ancestors.

The traditional life-style of the Lacandons is now being threatened. The jungle is rapidly being deforested for mahogany, and Maya from the land-poor Highlands follow in the wake of the loggers, burning out patches of jungle for cornfields. Many of the 400 remaining Lacandons have converted to evangelical Christianity; those who have not say that the reign of the God of Creation is over: the supreme god is now the Lord of Foreigners and Commerce.

OVERLEAF: Under the protection of the first bishop of Chiapas, the Highland Maya were shielded from the worst abuses of the conquistadores and enthusiastically joined the Catholic Church. The Maya call themselves *Batz'i Kristianoetik* ("True Christians") and have retained much of sixteenth-century Spanish ritual along with Pre-Columbian beliefs. Their faith is still strong; this church, in Nabenchauc, Zinacantan, was designed and built by the community in 1978.

ABOVE: Like the Ancestors who sit in judgment over life and death, civil officials and elders gather at the town hall to hear complaints and accusations. The man at the left occupies himself by plaiting palm for a hat while the litigants offer long and acrimonious accounts of their dispute. With the single exception of murder, all crimes are tried in local Maya courts.

OPPOSITE: Women from different communities rarely spoke to each other in the past, but the recent revival of folk art in Chiapas has given them more confidence and opened up new possibilities for travel. Here Rosha Hernandez, a leader of the weavers' society in San Andrés, listens to Juliana López, the most renowned potter of Amatenango, describe her experiences as a teacher.

OVERLEAF: A thin layer of topsoil barely covers the clay and limestone beneath it. This land was stripped of nutrients a hundred years ago, when Chamula was given to ranchers and the population forced to live in and feed themselves from one small area around Chamula center. Stone retention walls have recently been built to reclaim the eroded lands.

ABOVE: Strings of banners stretching from the bells of the church of Chamula to the walls of the atrium enclose the ritual space of the community, while a cloud of smoke rises behind the kiosk—the trail of a skyrocket shot off to announce the procession of religious officials emerging from the church. The patron of this festival stands before the church portal beside the two "bulls"—frameworks of fireworks carried over the heads of two dancing men. Black-robed civil officials holding their staffs of office watch the presentation from the kiosk.

OPPOSITE: A row of sticks plaited with rope of twisted grass serves as a temporary barrier until the branches planted in the low, mud-brick wall grow into a living fence.

ABOVE: Maya who marry outside of their community and go to live in the city abandon their traditional dress, culture, and language and become known as Ladinos, the name given to non-Indian Mexicans of Chiapas. Their children will speak only Spanish and will become indistinguishable from the majority of Mexicans.

OPPOSITE: Elders such as this man from Zinacantan personify the tradition that binds a Maya community together; they have lived long and survived many hardships, which have endowed them with the wisdom necessary to guide their community. Elders meet in council to advise on political and religious matters just as the Ancestors, supernatural beings who decide the fate of people who refuse to follow the proper path of life, meet in council on the sacred mountains. Members of the community adhere to these traditional beliefs or become outcasts, but men or women over fifty years of age have already proven their worth and are no longer required to follow the rules of behavior strictly. They can freely criticize civil and religious officials, drink without reproach, and wildly embellish their tales without losing the respect of their community.

ABOVE: Tojolobal-speaking Maya migrated to Chiapas from Guatemala in the seventeenth century and adopted European tuckwork and stitchery for their costumes. The women of Saltillo wear the most elaborate style of embroidered blouses. Children are dressed as small adults but are not considered to be fully human until they are seven or eight years old. For the first two years their souls are thought to be fragile and all too willing to return to heaven. Always close to their mothers, infants are quickly given a toy or milk at the slightest sign of crying, lest they become unhappy on this earth.

OPPOSITE: Each community has its own distinctive style of dress, which identifies its members. These women from Tenejapa are wearing their best *huipiles* for Sunday market. Each has composed the traditional designs in her own manner according to her personal taste and level of skill. These designs have been worn by Maya women for more than a thousand years, but the tradition remains alive due to constant innovations made within the framework of the ancient patterns. *Huipiles* draped on the statues of saints in churches and preserved for centuries are used as models; considered to be the finest of all *huipiles*, the standard by which all others are measured, they are studied by weavers who wish to learn the source of traditional designs.

OVERLEAF: Children over seven years old are expected to help the family with all the chores, but are never subjected to more work than they can handle. Here a woman from Chamula carries the heaviest load of flowers to market while her daughters follow with bundles of ornamental grasses and calla lilies.

ABOVE: Like most Maya, this Zinacantec shaman can identify almost every plant of the Highlands, but as a shaman he has received in his dreams special knowledge of which flowers and leafy branches should adorn the cross shrines at which he will pray for his patients' souls. He will also administer herbal cures, choosing specific plants to counteract illnesses that have been designated "hot" or "cold." Many of these plants are quite effective: the active ingredient in birth-control pills was discovered after study of an herb used by Maya women.

OPPOSITE: Agua Azul becomes saturated with lime and turns a deep blue color after flowing through the porous limestone caves of the Highlands. Natural causeways have been formed by the spread of limestone formations from logs petrified in the solution.

At Home

Like Venus, the Maya woman rises before dawn to begin her day's work. In the dark she rekindles the fire against the early morning chill, then starts grinding corn on a stone metate. Her house is made of interwoven sticks sealed with a mixture of mud and pine needles, the roof thatched with the long grass that grows in tufts on the hillsides, with posts and beams cut from oak and pine thickets found beyond the cornfields. Firelight flickers through cracks in the houses that flank the hillsides. The world is almost silent: only a faint *pat, pat, pat* can be heard repeating from each household as women all over the community press corn dough into flat, round cakes for their families' breakfasts.

Inside, a hot clay griddle, white with time, lies on the three hearthstones that circle the cooking fire. The hearthstones rest on the floor in the center of the house, directly under the peaked roof. Smoke from the cooking tortillas hangs in the air before it seeps through the blackened thatch. When a tortilla puffs up, a second woman, sister or daughter to the first, grabs it by the edge and flips it over. One by one the cooked tortillas are stacked in a hollow gourd lined with cloth to keep them warm.

The women are still busy stacking tortillas when the men—their husbands, brothers, sons, and grandsons who have built adjoining homes to form a family compound—rise, wash, and sit down at the small table for breakfast. Sweet, hot coffee waits for them there, along with beans or vegetables that lend flavor to the main food, tortillas. As the men eat their breakfast, the women fuss to make sure to serve them the freshest tortillas, the ones on top of the stack, adding more straight from the griddle. Each tortilla has been made with great care, for it is the Maya staff of life. A man cannot live without tortillas: a bachelor must depend on his mother or sisters to prepare his food; a widower or divorcé must remarry immediately if he wishes to eat like a man again.

OPPOSITE: Heavy woolen skirts and tunics are essential to the Chamula people, who live on the highest mountains of Chiapas. Sheep are treated as sacred animals, never to be slaughtered for food. Chamulas thank their sheep for their wool before shearing; afterward, they dress them in plastic raincoats to keep them warm until their fleece grows back. The statue of the patron saint of Chamula, John the Baptist, cradles a lamb in his arms, and ribbons placed on his hands are later made into necklaces for newborn lambs to protect them from harm.

The tortilla's importance to Maya life is reflected in the language. In Tzotzil a tortilla has many names, depending on when it was cooked, from what kind of corn it was made, and whose tortilla it is. A tortilla sitting in a gourd is a *vah*, but tortillas rarely sit long before someone eats them. Your tortilla is *avot*, and my tortilla is *kot*. If the tortilla was made the night before, it is a *vayemvah*, or "slept tortilla." A cooked tortilla left to dry out next to the fire is called *k'oshosh*; since these will keep for weeks without going stale, they are made for festivals and for men going off to work in the lowlands. A small, toasted tortilla is called *t'aha sat*. A tortilla made of fresh corn, rather than boiled dried kernels, is *ach' vah*; if the corn was young, *isis vah*. Each of these has a very different flavor, as do tortillas made of white, yellow, red, or black corn.

Classic Maya scene of a woman grinding corn while her husband relaxes with a cigar

Children who are slow to speak are given tortillas with a hole in the center, called *memelaetik*. If a girl does not want to make tortillas, three leaves of the *memela* tree are heated on the griddle and the hot leaves pressed between her hands as punishment for her laziness.

It was with a tortilla that Christ, or Kox, changed his older brothers into pigs, according to a story from Chenalhó. When Jesus was a little boy he had two older brothers who tormented him. One day he asked them to fetch some honey from a honeycomb on top of a big tree. While little Kox waited at the base of the

Our Holy Mother, from San Andrés

tree, his older brothers ate all the honey and threw down the wax. Kox shaped the wax into two gophers, which ate the roots of the tree, and down came the tree, killing his older brothers. Kox went home and asked his mother, the Virgin Mary, to make some small tortillas with holes in them. Then he returned to the tree and stuck the tortillas on his brothers' noses. They immediately revived and turned into pigs. The Virgin cried on seeing the pigs: "You have killed your brothers. Now what will become of us?"

Kox reassured his mother, saying, "I am going to see how many hills I can plant with maize." And so he went to work in the cornfields.

Men of the Maya household leave for the cornfields before sunrise. Although they may own only a small patch of land, each family grows some corn near its home. Fresh corn has golden red hair, like a newborn Maya child. Everyone must plant some corn to feel new life growing.

A cornfield yields more than corn. Twenty or thirty different vegetables and flowers may grow together in a single field. Beans are planted in the same raised mounds, to grow as the corn is harvested. Bean vines climb over the dead stalks, sprouting new leaves and red flowers. Squash vines stretch between the rows, their wide, flat leaves shading the ground. Yellow squash blossoms are delicious, and tender sprouts are added to soup. Herbs and wild greens are left to grow where they will.

Fruit trees are also planted near the house: peaches and apples in the Highlands, avocados below the frostline. Oranges, mangoes, bananas, and passion fruit grow in the tropical valleys. Dead trees support *chayote* vines. The whole plant is edible; the spiny *chayote* squash and its leaves are steamed and the white tuber dug up and eaten in the dry season. These fruits and vegetables are served as side dishes to the only true food—corn.

A Maya cornfield begins and ends as a forest. Corn eventually strips the soil of nutrients until the land must be left fallow. Over the years old cornfields become overgrown with tall pines as the soil regains its vitality. The best potential farmland is that covered with the oldest stand of woods.

The forest, a Chenalhó design

Clearing the woods, transforming a wild place into a domesticated one, is a task that Maya men today, as their heroes did before them, find daunting. The trees and animals resist the change. When little Kox went off to work he found that he could not keep his cornfields clear. The same story was told centuries earlier in the *Popol Vuh.* The Hero Twins discovered that the forest would reclaim its land each night:

They simply stuck their mattock in the ground, and the mattock simply cultivated the ground.

And it wasn't only the mattock that cultivated, but also the axe . . . felling all the trees and bushes, now leveling, mowing down the trees.

Just the one axe did it, and the mattock, breaking up thick masses, countless stalks and brambles . . . breaking up countless things, just clearing off whole mountains, small and great.

When they went on the second day and arrived at the garden, it had all grown up high again. Every tree and bush, every stalk and bramble had put itself back together again when they arrived. . . .

After that, they started the garden all over again. Just as before, the ground worked itself, along with the woodcutting. And then they shared their thoughts, there on the cleared and broken ground:

"We'll simply have to keep watch over our garden. Then, whatever may be happening here, we'll find out about it," they said when they shared their thoughts.

And there they took cover, and when they were well hidden there, all the animals gathered together, each one sat on its haunches, all the animals, small and great.

"Arise, conjoin, you trees!

"Arise, conjoin, you bushes!" they said. Then they made a great stir beneath the trees and bushes, then they came nearer, and then they showed their faces.

The first of these were the puma and jaguar. The boys tried to grab them, but they did not give themselves up. When the deer and rabbit came near they only got them by the tail, which just broke off; the deer left its tail in their hands. When they grabbed the tail of the deer, along with the tail of the rabbit, the tails were shortened. But the fox, coyote, peccary, and coati did not give themselves up.

A rabbit, from Chenalhó

These same animals attack the cornfields that have replaced the forest, gnawing on the corn each night. The wilderness is the Earthlord's domain; his creatures and trees attempt to halt the encroachment of civilization.

Unlike the Hero Twins, ordinary men cannot expect an axe and mattock to clear the forest for them; they must get up early each morning to chop trees into firewood. In Zinacantan the women gather fallen branches or cut down saplings and carry the burden home. In most other communities the men cut wood and bear the loads—up to 150 pounds—on their backs. With the wide strap of the tumpline pressing against their foreheads, their backs bent, the men trudge home down the mountain trails to stack the split logs against the house to dry.

Simple, four-wheeled wagons are used to haul wood in Amatenango. Amatenango is a pottery center that consumes a great deal of timber to fire the pots and water jugs that are sold throughout the Highlands. The hills surrounding Amatenango were denuded long ago, but fortunately a paved highway runs right past the town up to forested slopes a mile away. Boys chop the wood and stack it in the wagons, which they race like go-carts down the sides of the highway back to Amatenango.

In Chamula every tree has an owner. With one hundred thousand inhabitants, Chamula is so densely populated there are no wild forests left. Woodlands are cut selectively, with mature trees left for house construction. Large oaks are cut about five feet above the ground so that the trunks will sprout new shoots. These grow into a mass of thin stalks that are perfect for firewood and can be harvested over and over again.

There is not enough land in the Highlands to grow crops in amounts sufficient to feed the population, nor has there been for centuries. Even before the Spanish Conquest, the Maya never depended completely on the rugged mountain terrain for all their food. Maya communities extended down the slopes to the lowlands, a few hours' walk away. A Maya farmer would plant at least two cornfields, one in each region, so that his family could enjoy fresh corn for months. Even in times of drought they would be assured of some harvest.

Most Maya today are only part-time corn farmers, since few have enough land or access to land to feed their families and make a profit. Highland Maya rent sections of a lowland ranch to plant their corn, paying the owner a percentage of the crop. For a good part of the year the men must travel to distant cities to seek jobs as mason's assistants, to the lowlands to work as ranch hands, or to the Soconusco coast to pick coffee on the plantations. They may be away for months at a time, living in the heat and insect-infested tropics under primitive conditions and trying to save their meager wages to bring back home.

A woman's life seems to have changed very little over the ages. The men may be off working in the lowlands or weeding the cornfield, but the women stay home to cook, clean, and weave. A woman's role is not as mundane as it may appear, however; she participates in all religious rituals as an equal to her husband. In San Andrés a woman is called "the lord of the house," and her authority inside the house compound is unquestioned. The man is "the lord of the cornfields," but the corn he grows is not food until a woman transforms it into a tortilla.

The children imitate these roles at an early age. A boy about seven years old is considered a young adult. He takes his small hoe and joins his father and uncles in the fields, where he chops at a few weeds while his father explains which plants are good to eat and how to cut the roots of harmful weeds. His younger brother stays at home, rolling a hoop with a stick or growling like a truck as he pushes a block along a dirt path. The girls make tortillas out of leaves and mix up dirt and sticks in broken pots in a muddy imitation of a meal. Children also dance and sing like religious officials. They wonder what their spirit is like, what kind of animal reflects their soul and will be their companion spirit for the rest of this life. The following is a song of a five-year-old Chamula boy who imagines his cat is a jaguar, lord of the animal spirits:

iii iii iii
laa laa laa
Your tail is long, jaguar,
Your claws are long, jaguar,
I'm going to go, I'm going to go,
I'm going to go to the sky so that I will be happy.

Spotted animal,
Spotted jaguar,
My soul companion is a butterfly
because I fly around a lot in the air.

Lord of the earth
Lord of the heavens.
Lord of the sky
Lord of the woods.

Your paws are long, coyote,
Your legs are long, deer.
Your whiskers stand on end, jaguar.
Why are you looking at me?
Perhaps you are my soul companion.

Someday the child will see in his dreams the animal that corresponds to his personality and spirit.

Girls from El Bosque, a Chamula colony

The Maya may possess an animal spirit but they show little sentiment for wild animals and pets. Dogs are disdained for their habits and suffer constant abuse. Nevertheless they are fed, because it is believed that dogs carry dead souls across the river to the underworld. At midday the woman of the household will give the animal his daily tortilla and tell it to remember her when she dies.

Once the men have left for the cornfields the women store the leftover tortillas in a gourd and the balls of ground corn for the evening meal in a cloth bag hanging from a net so no animal can reach it. The fire is damped down, but a log is left smoldering to start the evening fire. The small table and chairs are placed on pegs against the wall, and the three-legged tortilla stand is tucked away. The hard dirt floor is swept clean. The chickens are chased outside, and their droppings scraped off the floor with a hoe. When the house is neat, the lord of the house begins the rest of her chores.

On sunny days she washes clothes. Carrying her laundry on her back, one child on top of the bundle and an infant in a cloth tied over one shoulder, she strides down to the riverbank. Perhaps her seven-year-old daughter will follow behind, carrying her little sister.

There are a dozen women by the water, pounding dirty clothes against flat stones, scrubbing them with soap until the white cloth sparkles. Pants and blouses, shawls and woolen tunics ripple across the grass and shrubs as they dry in the sun. Women and children wade out into the shallows, their wet skirts billowing around them as they splash water on their legs. No one swims, even if the water is deep enough. People bathe and wash clothes in the streams and rivulets below the mouth of springs, which are preserved for drinking water. The pools are precious, protected by fences from animals and guarded by small crosses from evil. Once a day a woman carries a clay jug to the water hole and exchanges news and gossip with the women from other households who share the same well.

A neighbor's sickness or sudden wealth may be discussed and analyzed to see if witchcraft is the cause. Tales of illicit or amorous adventures will spark a long conversation, especially if the case has been brought to court.

Scandal, gossip, slander, and eventually the truth emerge from testimony presented at court in epic form, the litigants speaking in couplets as they state their cases in exhaustive detail. The judges are elders from the community, men who have previously served as patrons of the festivals for the saints and as representatives of their hamlets in the civil government. They sit on a long bench under the portico of the municipal building facing the plaza, hearing cases and meting out a uniquely personal brand of justice. Trials are public; they give each side a chance to air its grievances before the community. A man being sued for divorce for beating his wife will be chastised, and the magistrate will try to convince the woman to give her husband one more chance. A person caught stealing will be given a fine and perhaps a few days in jail, but not before he has been publicly scolded by the magistrate. A woman in Chamula who finally admitted to stealing sheep earned this rebuke from the magistrate:

A political meeting in Zinacantan

You steal sheep
You steal chickens
You steal potatoes
You steal squash
You steal clothing
You steal cabbage
You steal turkeys
You steal anything.
The only thing you don't steal from people are
their testicles.
And those you only eat.

The woman was sentenced to a week of hard labor and a fine, but it was the final accusation (that she engaged in oral sex) that really stung. Such behavior is considered animalistic and must have caused some unusually lively gossip around the waterhole.

The whole day is not spent gossiping; there is too much work to be done. Most conversations are brief and formal unless they are with members of the immediate family or a *comadre*. Friends become honorary relatives, *comadres* and *compadres*, when one couple becomes baptismal godparents to another couple's child. *Comadres* are bound to help each other in times of need as well as to share tales of their neighbors.

When a woman returns home at midday she pours her water into a large clay pot in the far corner of the house. Now it is time to feed the chickens, which have been wandering through the fields and forest near the house all morning, scratching up grass and pecking at green leaves. Calling like a hen to her chicks, the woman sings out, *"t'ikt'ikte."* The chickens come running and flying in short leaps to the patio, where she has sprinkled handfuls of dried corn. As she checks for new eggs, the woman talks to the hens roosting in their nests, which are often made in broken cooking pots tied under the eaves.

The daily chores finished, she finally has time to weave. Weaving is both work and art. Maya women find it much more interesting than hoeing in the fields. The woman's backstrap loom has been waiting inside the house, rolled up and leaning against a wall. Once she sets the loom up on the patio, a woman, like her hens, is literally tied to the house. She hopes the children will not come up to her while she weaves. Maria Meza from Tenejapa explains:

If children come around, we must not let them pass under our loom. That's not good. We had better call it to their attention. There is a secret about this. If we let children get caught in our looms, they might get sick. There is another saying about this. If they put their heads in our loom, they will be big eaters, and will want to drink a lot of corn gruel. That's because the threads are primed in corn gruel. If they go under the loom, then our weaving will use up too much yarn and too much weft.

If a child's head appears through the delicate array of threads that stretch up from the loom, attached by a strap around the weaver's back, both mother and child are caught in the weave. But the mother is not as concerned about her work as much as for the safety of her child, who is never reprimanded for senseless behavior. For the first six or seven years of life a child's work is to play. Once a girl tires of making mud tortillas and weaving twigs and leaves she will patiently watch her mother weave and will be given a set of carved sticks so that she can play on a miniature loom. Some master the basic techniques when they are as young as three years old, but no child is expected to produce a usable piece of cloth until she is seven, when a mother will begin to correct and criticize her daughter's work.

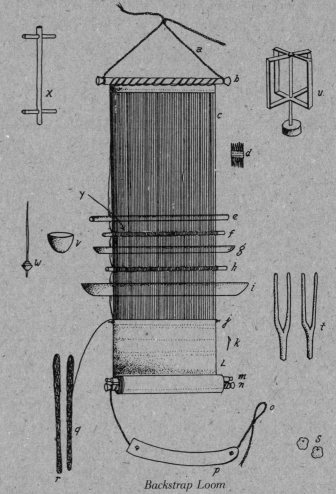

Backstrap Loom

a Cord fastened to tree or post	*n* Cloth beam
b Warp beam	*o* Cord fastened to backstrap
c Warp threads	*p* Backstrap
d Comb	*q* Bobbins
e Shed roll or shed stick	*r* Bobbins
f Heddle or heald rods	*s* Raw cotton
g Small batten	*t* Cotton beaters
h Heddle or heald rods	*u* Winding frame
i Large batten	*v* Gourd in which spindle
j Tenter	is spun
k Thorn used to fasten tenter	*w* Spindle
to web	*x* Warping frame
l Woven cloth or web	*y* Heald rod string
m Rolling stick	*z* Heading

From Donald Bush Cordry and Dorothy M. Cordry,
Costumes and Weaving of the Zoque Indians of Chiapas, Mexico

All women in the coolest areas of the Highlands learn how to weave the striped and plain white cloth that is used for tortilla napkins, shawls, men's shirts, and children's clothes. A generation ago all the clothing worn by the Highland Maya was handspun and woven, but now most men purchase collared

67

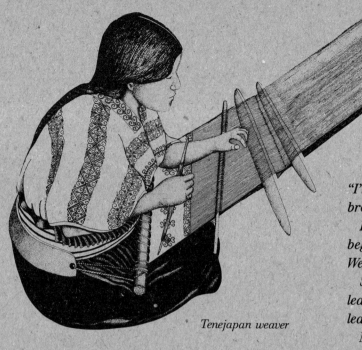

Tenejapan weaver

shirts to wear under their woven tunics, and turtleneck sweaters, worn under a *huipil*, have become an essential part of Tenejapan women's attire. Factory-woven cloth is used to tailor men's pants, and it is not uncommon for women to purchase this cloth for their *huipiles*, which are then embroidered to imitate the traditional woven designs. Although it takes as long to embroider a *huipil* as it does to weave one, a woman can embroider when it is impossible to weave. The starched threads of the loom stick together when the weather is humid, and the delicate weave of brocade can be seen only in bright sunlight.

Weaving plain cloth is child's work in comparison to brocade, in which colored yarns are carefully inserted into the cloth as it is woven to create designs. Most women know only a few designs, if any. A girl may learn brocade from her mother if she is lucky; if not, she may go to study with another relative who knows the designs. Brocade is not a simple process, but a creative act that requires patience, skill, and years of training. To master the art of brocade, says Slus Tonhol, a weaver from Tenejapa, a woman needs divine inspiration from the saints:

I learned to weave long ago. I was a young girl when I learned. "I'll never learn," I thought to myself.

"I'll probably die first here at this loom before I learn brocading!"

I was really sad that I didn't know how to weave. I began to pray. I prayed to Santa Luciá [Patroness of Weavers], to San Pedro, and to San Diego.

Slowly I began to learn. I went two or three times to leave candles at the church and pray. Then I began to learn little by little.

Now I know brocading very well. No one ever showed me how.

I learned with my heart.

At the beginning of the world the female saints taught the women of each village how to weave, and the saints remain the source of all skills and knowledge. Before beginning her first weaving, a girl offers candles to a saint and asks for assistance:

Look upon my poverty,
    Look upon my nakedness,
    Please.
Give me three graces,
    Three battens,
    Three heddles.
So I may weave my blouse,
    So I may weave my shirt,
    So I may weave my shawl.

In this weaver's prayer from Chamula, the girl asks for three battens and heddles instead of one because she will weave twill garments that use three different sheds. Each community has its own techniques and its own patron saint of weaving. Saint Rosario of Chamula inspires the girl to weave shawls and *huipiles* like those the women of her community wear and have worn for generations.

It is believed that the Catholic saints taught each community its distinctive style of dress. Although there is some European influence, particularly in the

Chamula shepherdess taking her muzzled flock to pasture

lowlands, Highland costume has its roots in Pre-Columbian culture. The brocaded *huipiles* of the Highlands resemble Classic Maya designs worn over twelve hundred years ago. When a woman weaves she is continuing in the path set down by her ancestors, confirming the validity of their teachings with her work.

The statues of the saints in each community are dressed in the costumes of their people. When the garments grow old, the sacristan may ask a woman known for her skill to weave new clothes for the sacred figures. From time to time female saints appear to women directly in dreams to request a new *huipil*. The woman must fulfill the dream or risk becoming ill. In San Andrés a woman will weave a saint's *huipil* as an act of devotion, just as young women in many communities will offer their first work to the patron saint.

Ceremonial costumes worn by married women are normally the most intricate weavings of the community, but young girls weave the brightest colors and most eye-dazzling designs. A serious weaver hopes to attract a husband with her craft. The men of Tenejapa, who wear elaborately brocaded costumes, will not marry a girl who cannot weave. "Don't fall in love with a girl if she doesn't know how to weave," they say. "What good will she be? Only if she knows the brocaded designs well, then will I want her. If she doesn't know how to weave, what clothing shall I wear? I couldn't very well walk around naked, now could I?"

Most weaving is done for the immediate family, but some women produce textiles for sale. Occasionally a woman may ask a relative who is an especially fine weaver to make her a blouse. Some weavers specialize in weaving garments for religious officials or special ceremonies. The wedding gown of Zinacantan, which has feathers woven into the breast and hem, is woven only by the women of two families, who sell or rent the gown to the bride.

Weavings are also sold to merchants in San Cristóbal de Las Casas, where tourism has recently become a major industry. Dozens of small shops sell simple, inexpensive weavings purchased at the lowest possible price from Maya women unable to sell their goods directly to tourists in the city. Members of Sna Jolobil, a Maya weavers' society, have been far more successful. With their own store in San Cristóbal, the weavers have learned how to run a business and raise the quality and price of Chiapas textiles.

Textiles are also sold from one community to another, especially the woolens woven in Chamula. In a Maya market a Chamula woman walks through the crowds with a wool shawl or man's tunic draped over her arm, a subtle announcement that it is for sale. A customer will hold the piece up to the sun to see how tightly it has been felted, discuss the quality of the wool, and bargain over the price. Wool is also sold in the market by women sitting in front of a mat with piles of cut fleece.

Chamula, San Andrés, and Zinacantan are the coldest communities and the only places in the Highlands where sheep are raised. Young girls bring the sheep out of their corral with muzzles over their mouths so they will not be tempted by a cornfield on the way to pasture. The girls bring their loom to the fields or spin wool while they watch the flock. Shepherdesses sitting alone in the hills are a grave temptation to young men, who otherwise never get a chance to speak to unmarried women. The shepherdesses, however, are rarely impressed when approached by a boy. After trying to ignore one boy's plea, a Zinacantec shepherdess cut him off, saying,

"Go see if you can find a companion for your lust. If you keep on blabbing here you'll be chased off with bullets by my father."

Some women never marry because they are "too haughty," independent, or simply do not care for men. Girls of poor families were once married off as early as twelve years old and often forced into marriages that they did not want. Women are freer to choose now and are waiting longer before looking for a husband.

"These girls who marry young have not had time to learn how to work. How will they eat?" said Lucia Gomez during a meeting of the weavers' society. "It is good to have a man, but when a woman has children, then she will learn hardship. I am studying weaving, learning how to work, so that if I have children I will know something valuable."

The women from Amatenango who support themselves selling pottery have the freedom to choose if they will marry or not. "Why should I marry a drunk?" asked a young woman from that community when I questioned why she remained single. "Now my friend here," she said, pointing to her embarrassed companion, "she's got a soft heart. She married a man."

The life of a single woman is not easy, but if she owns a little land or can sell her weaving or pottery she can get by. A man cannot eat if there is no woman in the house, but a woman can make her own tortillas. A man cannot hold any religious or political position unless he is married, but that is not the case for a woman. In Chamula unmarried women can serve as sacristans of Saint Rosario, and in Tenejapa the Holy Weaver must be a virgin. An unmarried or divorced woman lives with her family and helps her mother or sister make tortillas and clean house. If she earns any money, some will go for the corn she eats and the rest for thread for new clothes. Tortilla making is such hard work that having an extra hand is not a burden. In fact, it is quite common to have more than one woman in the kitchen.

Pottery of Amatenango

At dusk new wood is brought to the fire and the embers are blown into life again. The fragrance of *acote* pine floats in the air. Tamales made of cornmeal and bean paste wrapped in banana leaves have steamed for hours in a big cauldron. Beans have been bubbling in a small pot next to the log that has smoldered all day. The woman may fix candied watermelon squash, and if the family is wealthy they may have some meat or an egg; chickens are saved for festivals and curing ceremonies. Birds hunted by boys with slingshots may end up smoking over the fire, and if a cat shows off a field mouse it has caught, the mouse ends up smoked as well.

The whole family often comes together for dinner, when there is time to gossip and tell stories. The men who are not off working in the lowlands come inside to warm themselves by the fire while the tortillas are reheated and talk of local news, crops, the weather, or adventures of the neighbors. They crush a few dried chiles into the common bowl and scoop up beans in folded tortillas. As night settles someone mentions Don Foco, Mr. Flashlight, and everyone laughs.

There was a Zinacantec man who was sued for divorce because he once brought a flashlight to bed. His wife was outraged and accused him of sexual perversity. Women in Zinacantan never take off their skirts, even to wash themselves. A fresh skirt is placed over the soiled one before it is taken off to be washed. And of course they go to bed wrapped in yards of blue skirt. After fourteen years of marriage the poor man wanted to see all of his wife. That, she protested, was going too far! The man was summoned to court and his wife left him.

While the family is still gathered by the fire, an owl calls, causing some arrest. Perhaps it is a witch come to steal someone's soul. There are demons that wander in the night, black men with wings who steal women for their wives. Women who are alone while their husbands are working at some distant labor are the main prey of the Spook. A relative may stay with her at night, and she will keep in close contact with her closest neighbors, who are usually her *comadres* and *compadres*.

Before going to bed, the woman leaves a bucket of shelled corn mixed with lime water simmering by the fire. She is careful to add just the right amount of water; too much may cause the pot to boil over and put out the fire, and she will wake to find half-cooked corn, unusable for the morning tortillas. Or she may discover a Spook, according to a story from Zinacantan:

Once there were many Spooks. The women's husbands weren't around. They had gone to the lowlands to farm.

They slept at dusk.

"Comadre, will you listen for me and tell me if my corn boils over? I won't know because I am going to sleep at the fireside," said the woman.

"All right, I'll probably hear it," said her comadre. She hears it hissing now. "Comadre, comadre, your corn is boiling over," she said.

But it was the woman's blood. The Spook was there. "The corn is ready, Com-a-dre!" said the Spook.

In the night the other side of reality comes forth. When a person dreams, his soul leaves his sleeping body on the surface of the earth. In some dreams the person's soul may meet a witch in the guise of a bull or a devil that has left his flesh on a cross to wander about as a bloody skeleton. If a person's soul is strong

A late Classic figure from Jaina of a Maya woman at her loom

it will defeat the demons and return whole to the earth's surface; otherwise, the person may die. Dreams may predict that a man will lose his mule or that he will finally find a wife. A powerful dreamer may wander to the mountain shrine of the Ancestors and there learn how to cure the sick.

The saints who walked the earth at the beginning of time are still present in dreams. They have not abandoned their people, the Maya, who remain faithful to their teachings. A Maya man clearing a forest for cornfields knows that he is continuing the work begun by God. In times of drought the Virgin will appear in dreams to announce the creation of a new lake in a dry valley, a manifestation of her power that has often come to pass. If a ritual has been forgotten the saints tell the people in dreams how the festivals should proceed. The female saints, who were the first to weave the designs of each community, come back in dreams to show women how the patterns of creation can be woven into their *huipiles*. If it is woven without a flaw, the *huipil* is considered to be well dreamt.

The hidden part of daily life, the Maya learn and live in their dreams.

The Lord's Work

Corn—God's holy sunbeams—surrounds and sustains each Maya home. The four colors of corn correspond to the cardinal directions in an ancient vision of the world. The Maya stand at the center of the world, in the color yash—*the color of blue sky, gray mist, and green stalks of sprouting corn.*

Planting corn, making tortillas, and other tasks of Maya life are sacred duties that recall the acts of God and the Ancestors. The Hero Twins of Maya mythology cleared the forest for cornfields, and later stories tell how the Christ child worked in the field to support His mother. The Virgin made Christ tortillas, just as Maya women do for their families every day. The saints wove huipiles *and tended their flocks of sheep when they walked upon the earth. In each daily chore the Maya follow the path laid down at the beginning of time.*

ABOVE: Zinacantec men turn the thin topsoil by hand to prepare a field near their home for corn planting before the rains begin to fall in May. Metal has long replaced ancient stone implements, but the hoe remains a basic tool in the Highlands, where most land is too steep and rocky to plow.

OPPOSITE: Maya women own land and often work in the fields when there are not enough men in the household. Although corn is sown to coincide with the rains, Chamulas hand-water their vegetable patches during the dry season to provide an extra cash crop to sell in the market center at San Cristóbal de Las Casas.

OVERLEAF: Cornstalks in the fields surrounding Chamula homes are bent to allow the ears to dry before they are stored in a bin in the corner of the house. The best ears are hung from the rafters to provide the next year's seed.

ABOVE: On top of her net bag of goods a Chamula woman carries a load of calla lilies to market. Easily grown in marshy areas near springs or in cornfields next to the house, where they can be watered by hand, calla lilies are a cash crop for Maya women.

OPPOSITE: A young Ladina girl in the San Cristóbal market sells flowers she and her mother purchased earlier in the day from Maya farmers. Flowers are a major business in Chiapas; almost every Mexican home has a small house altar decorated with blossoms. Zinacantecs, who specialize in raising carnations, gladiolus, and other temperate-climate flowers, bring them directly to market in the tropics, where they fetch a better price.

OVERLEAF: Chamula vegetable farmers display their cabbage crop while Ladina women wearing aprons and dark shawls seek bargains in the open market of San Cristóbal. All the vegetables in the market once came from Chamula, which is just on the other side of the mountain ridge behind the market.

ABOVE: A Chamula girl carrying her younger sister on her back sells bundles of *acote* she gathered from the forest to a Ladina merchant. *Acote*, a resinous pinewood, burns like a torch and is used to start cooking fires.

OPPOSITE: Round cakes of mineral salt from the wells at Salinas and Ixtapa sold by Zinacantec merchants were the only source of salt in the Highlands for centuries. Zinacantec salt sellers are still seen in every market. Before commercially dyed yarns were available in Chiapas, the salt sellers' wives were the principal source of wool dyed red with dried cochineal insects; they still accompany their husbands to market but have now turned to selling apples or peaches.

OVERLEAF: Although in most communities gathering firewood is a man's task, in Zinacantan women split oak saplings and carry them home from the woods. The wood is cut into long pieces so that the cooking fire can be more easily controlled: arranged like spokes of a wheel, the sticks are pushed forward to increase the flames and pulled back to dampen the fire.

ABOVE: Clothing is beaten clean on smooth stones of the river running through the Chenalhó valley. Tap water is available in community centers, but most women wash in streams and carry drinking water home daily from mountain springs.

OPPOSITE: During a free moment, a Zinacantec woman combs out the tangles in her hair before rebraiding it. Long hair is a luxury that is tended with great care. Women plait bright ribbons into their braids to accent the deep black color of their hair and tie the two ends together so that the braids will not flip forward as they work.

ABOVE: Maya women wake up hours before sunrise to make their family's daily supply of tortillas. Here a Zinacantec girl is reaching to pluck a finished tortilla from the clay griddle on the fire while leaning on the tortilla press with her other hand.

OPPOSITE: Xunka Tulan of Nabenchauc checks her pot of simmering corn before going off to bed. The kernels will be left on the embers all night long to cook slowly in a solution of lime water; the lime fixes the nutrients in the corn and softens the shells so that the corn can be easily ground into dough the next morning.

OVERLEAF: A Zinacantec family, all immaculately dressed for travel, prepare to leave their single-room house, which serves as granary, closet, and cookhouse as well as bedroom and living area. The mother, about to fling a shawl over her back, will deftly catch her daughter in its folds. By tying the corners of the shawl in a knot at her chest, she can carry her child comfortably on her back and keep her warm throughout the journey; the wrap can also be adjusted to allow the child to ride in front while being breast-fed.

ABOVE: The Tulan home in Nabenchauc, like most Maya households, appears to be self-sufficient, as wood, clay, and other natural materials are abundant. There has always been a lively exchange of goods and services among neighbors, however. Now *tak'in*, the Tzotzil word for metal and money, has replaced barter in the marketplace, where even the most isolated of families purchase metal tools and plastic buckets along with pottery and baskets made by specialists from other communities.

OPPOSITE: A Zinacantec man descends from his perch in a pine tree after cutting off the top of the pine, seen lying in the branches below. When he gets home he will plant the trunk in the floor near the hearth, where it will serve as a rack for clean pots hanging off its branches.

OVERLEAF: Only a single tuft of thatch grass remains on a hillside cropped closely by sheep. Chamula women have the right to graze their flocks on any land left fallow, but they must watch their sheep lest any wander into nearby cornfields.

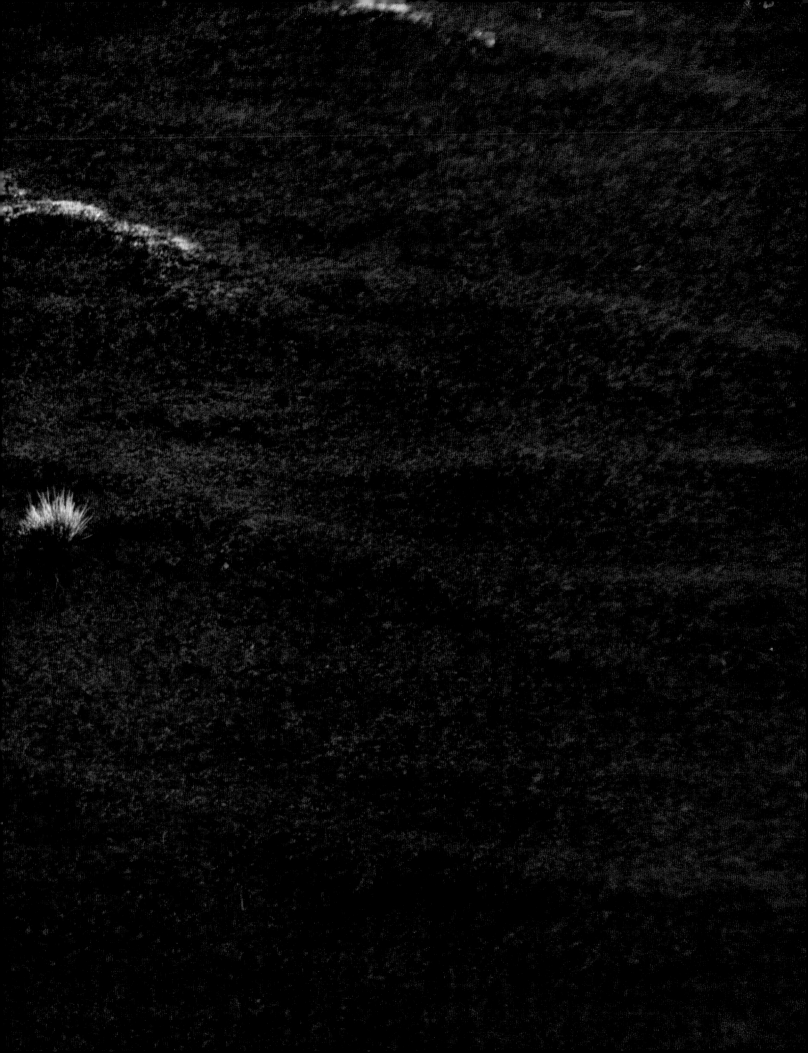

THESE PAGES: It is said in Chamula that when God invented the guitar the devil created the violin to do him one better. The violin being made by the Zinacantec man (above), like all Zinacantec violins, will have only two strings but will otherwise be almost identical to the fifteenth-century Spanish ravel. The harp and guitar played in Tenejapa (opposite) are also faithful reproductions of colonial instruments. Each Maya community has its own trios of harpist, guitarist, and violinist, all men who received inspiration in dreams to become "musicians for life." The melodies they play are derived from choral music taught by friars centuries ago.

OVERLEAF, LEFT: A long, flat braid of palm is sewn into a spiral, starting at the center, to form a man's hat. Only this one elder in Amatenango still wears palm hats, which have gone out of fashion in his community. On ceremonial occasions, however, the traditional *pixobal* remains an essential part of the ritual attire.

OVERLEAF, RIGHT: The image of a Spanish conquistador becomes a Carnaval mask in Ocozocoautla. The carved cedar will last for generations, but the lacquered and painted surface is likely to be damaged in the raucous celebration, which keeps most Maya mask makers busy retouching scraped noses and fallen eyelashes for months afterward.

ABOVE: Three generations of potters in Amatenango, where the women produce most of the traditional water jugs used throughout the Highlands as well as commercial pottery for tourists, sort through small figures of animals, made by the youngest girls to practice working with clay. The dried *animalitos* and flowerpots are carefully arranged on an open area where a fire is built around them as an open kiln.

OPPOSITE: Pottery production leaves little time for weaving in Amatenango. Women there purchase woven cloth from neighboring communities and embroider it with wide loops of herringbone stitch that is later tacked down with a sewing machine. The pattern is simple, but each *huipil* is individualized with additional colored stripes or flowers embroidered along the border.

OVERLEAF: In most Highland communities, weaving is an integral part of each woman's life. A woman becomes part of her loom; the wide strap across her lower back holds the warp strings taut. Here Rosha Hernandez of San Andrés weaves a brocaded *huipil*, similar to the one she is wearing, which will take her several months to complete. After she has finished her work for the day, Rosha will take the loom off, roll it up, and store it inside the house before the afternoon rains fall.

The Daughters of the Earthlord

The design of the universe is woven, with clarity and purpose, line by line into Maya cloth. The weaver maps the motion of the sun through the heavens and the underworld, through time and space. Through the repetition of the universe design the lordly sun is prompted to continue his journey. A Maya woman weaves the cosmos as it awakens.

Below the design of the world the Earthlord and his musician, the toad, dance in the cotton weave. On the flower design that covers the sleeves sits a scorpion, a being that attracts rain. Through these characters the weaver has set the scene for a central drama. While the toad sings at the mouth of the Earthlord's moutain cave, the Earthlord's daughters prepare cotton, which will be transformed by a bolt of lightning into rain clouds. The scorpion is introduced into their midst to prick the lightning into action. The cotton *huipil*, perfectly animated, draws the powers that bring life-sustaining rain.

A Maya woman weaves her own vision of the sacred universe and signs her works with a personal design. There are a variety of styles that identify the weaver's community, but all ceremonial *huipiles* portray the world as a diamond. The four sides of the diamond represent the boundaries of space and time; the smaller diamonds at each corner, the cardinal points. East is above, where the sun emerges. West is below, the end of the day. North is on the left, because for the Maya north is insignificant; in the tropical skies the sun passes directly overhead, angling only slightly toward the north or south in different seasons. At night the stars also move directly from east to west, undistorted by Polaris, which lies near the horizon.

When the sun rises and sets it passes through the oceans, the Caribbean Sea in the east and the Pacific to the west. These watery boundaries are represented in the universe design by indigo blue threads. Some say the sun boils and evaporates the seas to keep the waters from flooding the earth again.

OPPOSITE: Combining an ancient technique with modern acrylic yarns, Maruch Tulan of Nabenchauc, Zinacantan, inserts white chicken feathers into the brocade of a wedding *huipil.* Featherwork was once a widely practiced art—Aztec rulers used to keep aviaries to supply feathers for their clothing—but now the members of the Tulan family and a few other women in Zinacantan are the only feather weavers left in all Mexico and Central America.

The universe design: the four small diamonds indicate the cardinal directions; a narrow line connects east, at the top, and west, at the bottom, to show the path of the sun

When the sun sets it travels below the earth and becomes the Lord of the Night. On the other side of the world the night sun passes close by a land of dwarfs, who wear thick mud hats to protect themselves from its unbearable heat.

In the universe design the path of the sun across the sky is shown by a thin yellow line connecting the small diamonds of the east and west to a large central diamond. This inner diamond has curls on each side that represent wings; called *pepen*, "butterfly," it is the weavers' symbol for the day sun. The butterfly is

used as a metaphor for the sun because it too becomes an inhabitant of the underworld when day turns into night. Butterflies and fruit bats—inhabitants of caves, considered to be the portals of the underworld—feed on the same flowers in the Highlands. In the faint light of dusk one can see a butterfly fluttering among the bushes alongside a cornfield and then see a bat flying away from the same spot.

The sun is personified as Our Lord, Jesus Christ;

the moon is Our Holy Mother, the Virgin Mary; and the stars are the glowing crowns of the saints. The sun, the moon, and the stars all follow a path across thirteen layers of sky and nine layers of night. Storytellers say the sun crosses the sky as a man climbs across a roof. At each hour it passes another layer, until at noon it is at the peak. There it pauses for a moment before descending across the other side of the sky.

The universe design shows the sun at noon, resting in the center of its daily journey. To represent the sun in motion, *huipiles* repeat row after row of diamonds, with small variations. The ninth and thirteenth row of *huipiles* from the community of Magdalenas are marked with a dark line or a change of color to indicate the division between the underworld and the sky. Since the layers can be described as hours, the movement through space is also movement through time. The repetitions of the universe design show the sun's daily and yearly motion.

The yearly cycle can be represented in two ways. Some weavers in Magdalenas make color changes on the eighteenth, twentieth, nineteenth, and fifth rows to mark the eighteen months of twenty days and the nineteenth month of five days that comprise the Maya calendar. Weavers in San Andrés illustrate the solstice by placing a bright yellow spot along the side of the path of the sun—at the tip of the wing of the butterfly—to signify the sun's deviation from its nor-

Rosha Hernandez of San Andrés spinning wool. The brocaded patterns that cover the sleeves, front, and back of her huipil form an open cross, with Rosha in the center

Lady Xoc of Yaxchilán

mal path. Each row of diamonds will have a bright spot first on one side, then on the other side of the sun's path, to show winter and summer solstice.

When a Maya woman puts on her *huipil* she emerges through the neckhole symbolically in the axis of the world. The designs of the universe radiate from her head, extending over the sleeves and bodice of the *huipil* to form an open cross with the woman in the middle. Here the supernatural and the ordinary meet. Here, in the very center of a world woven from dreams and myths, she stands between heaven and the underworld.

The embodiment of time and space in a field of diamond-shaped designs has been a sacred concept since the Classic Maya period. Lady Xoc of Yaxchilán wore this same motif in A.D. 709 when she performed the bloodletting ritual described previously. The ritual and the gods have been suppressed in the last twelve hundred years of Maya culture, but the Maya world and the Maya image of the universe that is woven into the cloth have remained unchanged.

When Lady Xoc has a vision of a royal supernatural emerging from the jaws of a great serpent, as portrayed on the second of the Yaxchilán lintels, she wears a *huipil* with the open-cross design cut out of the cloth in imitation of the open mouth of the earth monster. The earth, the reptilian monster, the vision serpent, and the caves that were the entrances to the underworld were all represented in Classic Maya art as quatrefoils. The portal between the worlds has retained its form as an open cross, although the beings that inhabit the underworld have changed shape with time. The earth is no longer represented as a huge reptilian monster; now, however, a toad stands guard at the entrance to the Earthlord's cave in myths and weaving.

Toads are pervasive in Classic Maya art. The toad design appears on the *huipil* of the queen of Yaxchilán in the final scene as a symbol of the fecundity of the reign of her husband, Shield Jaguar. The amphibious toad remains a symbol of the fertility of the earth, and of the waters that gave it birth.

A toad called Antonia waits at the door and guards the Earthlord's house in a tale from Chenalhó. In a Chol version of the same myth the toad is the Earthlord's wife. And in Zinacantec myth the toad is the Earthlord's musician; it sings at the mouths of caves. According to Anselmo Perez, a Zinacantec shaman, the toad is the Earthlord's shaman. This toad, called *Henhen* in Tzotzil and *Bufus marinus* by biologists, exudes as a defense mechanism a score of chemicals from glands on its skin. Many of the chemicals are deadly poisons; one is thought to be an anesthetic fifty times as strong as cocaine, another is a powerful hallucinogen. Someone who kisses this toad and survives the experience actually may see a prince.

The Earthlord is both evil and beneficent. He is the lord of purgatory, where, in payment for their sins, souls must labor as debt peons on his underworld plantation. He can also be generous: he is the master of wind, water, thunder, and rain and can make the earth blossom.

In weavings the Earthlord is surrounded by flowering plants. Among the flower designs a sinuous line wiggles across the weave in the path of a snake. As

The snake path, a simple curling line, becomes a row of flowering plants

the following Zinacantec story illustrates, the snake's path leads to the underworld:

Once there was a Chamulan who was hunting on the trail to the lowlands. A snake appeared and stretched in the middle of the path. Quickly he slashed it with a machete. . . .

"Please, my Chamulan," said the snake, "won't you be so kind as to carry me home? I'll show you where it is if you will carry me away. It won't be for nothing. My father will give you any payment you want," said the snake, the thunderbolt.

It was no ordinary snake. The pieces piled themselves up on the trail. The Chamulan carried them off.

They walked on and on until they reached a cave. The fog was thick.

"I can't see at all," said the Chamulan.

"It's just a cloud," said the snake. "The cloud will rise. We go down this path. My house is just a bit further." They followed the path.

"Knock on the rock. This is my house." The man knocked. The snake's father opened the door.

"Sir," said the Chamulan, "is this your son you see wounded to death? I've come to bring him back to you."

"Yes, that's my boy. Thank you for bringing him to me. How much do I owe you?" the father asked.

"You don't owe me anything, sir," the Chamulan said. He laid the snake down on his bed.

In a San Andrés version of this tale the man spies four young women fluffing cotton in the back of the Earthlord's cave. Although Yusum, as he is called, had at first refused payment for returning the snake, the sight of the women makes him change his mind: "Well, perhaps a wife. I might take one of your daughters."

"Of course," said the Earthlord. "But you must wait a bit. We are going to have a little festival now. Anhel (lightning) is going to arrive soon. You can't watch. It will kill you to watch. So stick your head in the ground and wait a bit."

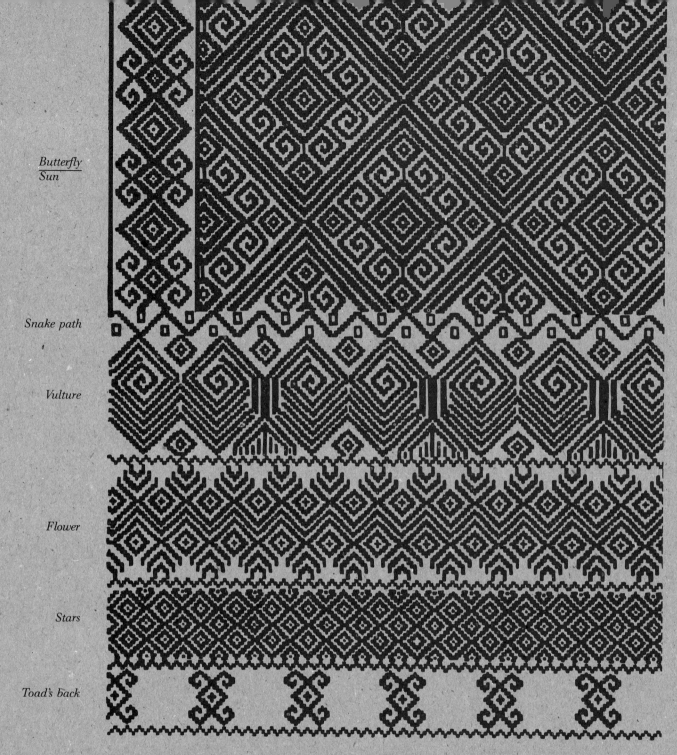

Butterfly / Sun

Snake path

Vulture

Flower

Stars

Toad's back

The butterfly/sun design in the diamonds that cover a Magdalenas huipil is repeated along the side with alternating diamonds and butterflies to show the path of the sun. Below these designs, a row of small rectangles between the zig-zag of the path of the snake indicates that the weaver has held religious office. The three vertical lines in the designs below form the body of a vulture, the symbol of the community of Magdalenas. A row of chevron-like "flowers" is above a field of diamonds that represent stars. At the base of the brocade is the weaver's signature pattern—the back of a toad.

The huipil places the weaver in the center of the universe and names her as an individual, a member of the community, and one who has served the saints. Wearing this huipil she will pray to the saints—the stars in heaven—and to the Earthlord that the world may follow her design and flower.

Anhel arrived and the lightning and thunder filled the cave. Yusum took just a little peek and saw the cotton grow higher and higher and turn into clouds.

The flash of lightning that transforms the cotton into clouds almost kills Yusum, but he recovers and takes one of the Earthlord's daughters as his wife. In the Chenalhó version of this story Yusum is very lazy and has planted only a few stalks of corn. When the Earthlord's daughter picks a few ears for their dinner they magically multiply and fill her net bag, for she is also the Mother of Corn. Yusum, thinking that his new wife has stripped the field bare, hits her on the nose. When she wipes her bloody nose with an ear of corn, it turns red, and that is the origin of red corn. The woman leaves him and returns to her father's cave. Yusum then visits the Earthlord to beg his forgiveness. His father-in-law tells him, "You are going to be of service. You will go from one place to another." Yusum becomes a bolt of lightning, an *anhel*, so called because lightning is like angels that dance in the clouds.

On a *huipil* the designs of the Earthlord, snakes, and toad are brocaded with colored yarns onto white cotton cloth. The universe design completely masks the cotton base of the weave but around the figures of the underworld there is space to show the white cotton clouds.

In the Magdalenas *huipil* the sleeves are covered with rows of flowering plants bordered by snakes. Below them are toads and the Earthlord, holding flowers. Hidden among the plants is the long, spiny tail of the scorpion. According to another story from

Chenalhó, the scorpion once bit the penis of Anhel. Anhel, in retribution, has forced the scorpion to live under rocks in hiding from the lightning bolts that Anhel hurls at him. The weaver has placed the scor-

pion on the *huipil* to goad the lightning, to bring about that moment when the white cotton of her garment will attract the powers that cause the rain. As a weaver the woman is aligned with the daughters of the Earthlord and the inhabitants of his cave that replenish the earth.

The underworld, the heavens, and the earth were created, according to Classic Maya texts, trillions of years ago. Since then the world has been destroyed and recreated many times. Ancient texts cite 3114 B.C. as the beginning of the present creation; the Maya of Chiapas say that this world began after the Flood destroyed the previous one. God and the saints walked upon the new earth and established the Maya communities as they are today.

Different aspects of the story of the Flood are woven into each community's *huipiles*. Designs with three posts in the center placed on the lower edge of the brocade symbolize characters from the story.

The community design of Magdalenas is a vulture. The three lines are its body, the diamond above is its head, and the lines that spiral from the sides of the body are its wings, spread out as the bird suns itself at dawn. In the Maya myth Noah sent out many different kinds of birds to seek dry land, but none returned. Then he sent a dove. When the dove, which had not eaten for forty days, came across land and saw all the corpses, it swooped down and began to eat them. At that moment the dove was transformed into a vulture.

Another myth relates how Christ punished the unrepentant survivors of the Flood:

Those who were saved could see Our Lord. When Our Lord himself came down to look, all those who were saved were angry.

"How did you escape?" Our Lord asked.

"We climbed to the mountain top," some said. "We fled to the woods," said others.

"Where? What woods?"

"Wherever there are any," they answered.

"And your houses?" he asked.

"Oh, who cares!" they said.

"What did you live on?"

"We didn't live on anything much. We lived on vine berries. We lived on nuts." They talked back angrily now.

"Do you want to go on living?" asked Our Lord. "Well, look behind you then."

When they looked behind them, their tails appeared. They were turned into monkeys.

Monkeys are the people of long ago. Their faces look human except that they have fur. They have fur and long tails and live in the forest because they didn't obey Our Lord's command.

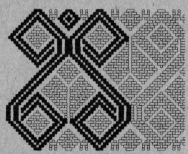

The monkey figures in the designs of both San Andrés and Chenalhó. In San Andrés the three posts are its body, and the lines that curl from these three central lines are its long arms and legs. The Chenalhó design represents the forest where monkeys and demons and other wild creatures live. The three posts are the trees, and the multiple curls are vines intertwined with bromeliads and sprouting plants.

Vultures, monkeys, and other wild creatures represent the chaotic world, the opposite of community. They remind people of the destruction that will come again if immoral behavior reigns.

In San Andrés there is a variation of the three post design called Father-Mother. This represents the An-

cestors, those who survived the Flood and remained human by obeying the Lord, clearing the forest, and planting corn. The three posts are the Father's body and refer to the house that he rebuilt. The Mother has the multiple arms of a corn plant. The Fathers-Mothers are the root and guardians of society.

The Ancestors and the saints are allies. Both established the rules of proper behavior at the beginning of the world. The saints came after the Flood to organize the communities and build the churches. Me' Abrila of Magdalenas tells of the arrival of her community's patron saint:

Our Mother Magdalena came here looking for a place to live. She was looking for open land. She climbed a cedar tree to see better, a cedar with large limbs. She secured herself to the tree with resin and set up her loom. She looked and saw that the land was without fault.

"It is good, the water and everything here is good," said Our Mother. She decided to make her house here, to build her church.

There in the tree she was weaving, she was brocading her designs. Her daughters learned a little because Our Mother knew how to do it herself. They could weave very well then, they say, tight and straight.

Mary Magdalene weaving in a tree

When Mary Magadalene founded the community of Magdalenas her first act was to weave herself a *huipil*. The costumes of each community identify its people as descendants of its patron saint. According to Me'Abrila, "Santa Marta wears the same *huipil* as Magdalena because they are members of the same family."

In Magdalenas each statue of a saint wears layers of *huipiles*, the oldest one next to the saint's body. In a place without libraries or museums the saints' wardrobes are the sacred repositories of traditional designs. The saints are the first and the finest weavers of the community, and their clothing is a model for present-day weavers. Margarita Vasquez Gomez of Magdalenas describes studying the saints' *huipiles*:

When I learned how to weave, I went three times to speak with the Virgin. I asked her to teach me, to put knowledge in my head and in my heart, because I liked her clothes and wanted to wear the same. I made three weavings, just samplers, which I gave to our Holy Mother. Each time I cried and cried because I wanted to learn, and then I returned home to weave. I studied the Virgin's huipil *carefully inside and out to see how it was made. . . . But it is not easy to learn, you only see a little and remember less.*

Each saint is bathed once a year on her feast day. Her coin necklaces are counted to make sure that none is missing, and the ceremonial *huipiles* are washed in rose water and censed by a *Martoma*, a patron of the saint's annual festival. The saint's *huipiles* are laid out in a long row to dry, and the townspeople come to kiss the hem of her garments and drink the rose water. When a *huipil* becomes too ragged with age for the saint to wear, it is placed in a coffer with the saint's other possessions to be kept in the *Martoma*'s house.

The care of the saints' clothing preserves the oldest examples of weaving. Under the yards of gaudy prints covering Santa Rosario in Chamula was a silk brocaded *huipil* that had been washed and incensed over one hundred times. When the *huipil* became threadbare a few years ago, the sacristan of the church searched for a woman to reproduce the old designs and weave a new *huipil* for the saint. Santa Rosario's conservative new clothes will adorn the statue for another century.

The saints have worn *huipiles* since the colonial period, when Dominican friars asked Maya weavers to dress the saints, as was the custom in Spain. Statues of Maya gods were clothed before the conquest: Maya weavers simply continued the practice, now dedicating their most intricate work to adorn new statues of pale white women and bearded men. But gone now were the laws prohibiting the Maya people from wearing the same *huipiles* as the deities and Maya royalty. After the conquest the ancient and holy designs could be worn by all Maya. The remarkable continuity in women's costume over the last 450 years is a result of their having studied the old *huipiles* of, and weaving new ones for, the saints.

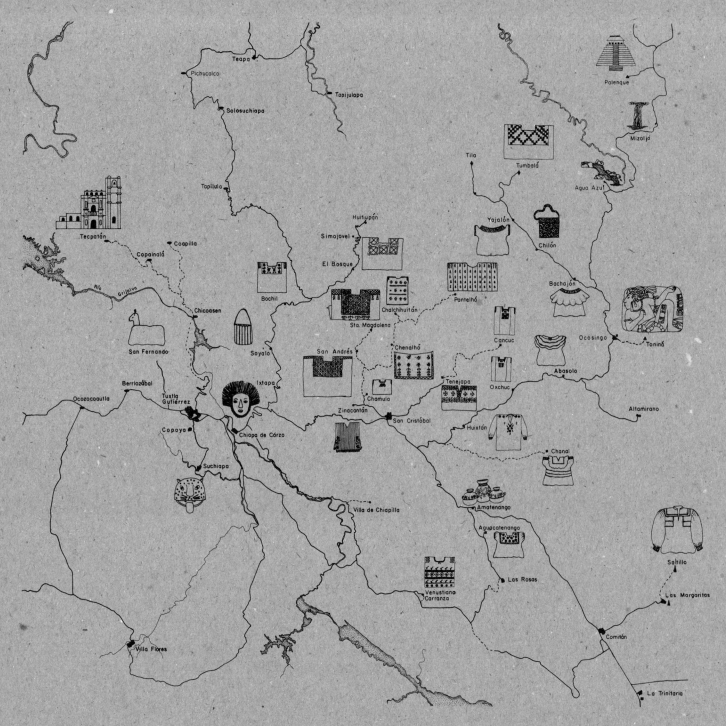

The Highlands of Chiapas

The costume of Maya men has changed more radically. Their daily attire now combines elements of Pre-Columbian and Spanish dress. The ancient loin cloth is now worn as a sash, tied around short pants that were introduced in the colonial period. The wool and cotton tunics that most men in the Highlands wear today are similar to tunics worn by Spanish knights and sleeveless shirts worn by Maya warriors. In Chamula a white wool tunic is worn under a long, black coat; the outfit looks much like the Dominicans' wool habit.

Maya nobles adopted Spanish attire immediately after the conquest. Eventually this proved to be too expensive, for the Spaniards preferred imported linens and costly silks. Sixteenth-century-style costume is still worn today by religious officials on ceremonial occasions.

Women's costume also shows some outside influence. After the Aztec troops that accompanied Bernal Díaz and the other conquistadores to Chiapas settled in San Cristóbal, the neighboring communities of Zinacantan and Chamula adopted Aztec styles of dress, although Chamula retained traditional Maya garb for ceremonial garments. Interestingly, the descendants of the Aztecs no longer wear these fifteenth-century fashions; Zinacantan is the last place in Mexico to continue the Aztec practice of weaving feathers into *huipiles.*

In the nineteenth century, when Indians were virtual slaves and had little time or money to weave, those who worked in the lowland cattle ranches and coffee plantations adopted the European peasant costumes. Frilly embroidered blouses are still worn by Tzeltal and Tojolobal women.

European influence was not as strong in the Highlands. Weavers there were inspired by dreams to revive the art of Maya design. At the turn of the twentieth century the women of Tenejapa had completely forgotten how to brocade. When their patron saint of weaving, Saint Luciá, appeared to each of three Tenejapan women and asked them to weave a

*Classic Maya man
from the court of Bonampak*

115

Tenejapan religious officials: the woman's huipil
is the same as that worn by Santa Luciá

brocaded *huipil*, they were unable to comply. All three women tried to refuse, and all became ill for not following the saint's commands. Eventually the women went to Chenalhó and to San Andrés to study brocade, and they finally brought back a *huipil* for the saint. Other women studied this *huipil*, and a weavers' society was formed to weave for the saints and to teach other women how to brocade. Gradually, Tenejapa developed its own style. Over the years designs and costumes became more complex, and the Highlands are experiencing a creative renaissance in weaving.

Maya weavers currently believe that designs were taught "at the beginning of the world by Our Holy Mother." And it is essentially true that despite minor changes, the patterns woven into the saints' *huipiles* are the same as those that appear in depictions of textiles dating from the beginnings of Maya culture.

Weavers recognize the antiquity and sanctity of woven motifs and are reluctant to talk about their meaning. Consequently, the same design may have up to four different kinds of names, each reflecting a different perspective. Some weavers name a design on the basis of where it is placed in the *huipil*. A three-post community design, which appears at the lower edge of the brocade, may be called "edge design," for example. Another weaver may name the same design on the basis of technique—"five warps," for instance, or "seven warps," depending on the number of warp threads between two critical points in the brocaded design. This same design may also be named for a particular element in it, in this case "posts design," because of the three vertical lines in the center. Or, as we have seen, the design may be called "monkey," "vulture," "Ancestors," or whatever else it may represent. This last example is the most interesting and meaningful but at the same time the most difficult to elicit. Only a few weavers know how to truly name, not just describe, the motif, although most Maya women know their mythology. They can name the basic designs, such as the toad, a prominent player in the myths. When I asked the weavers, "Why a toad?" the response was invariably, "It's custom, that's the way it's always been."

I could not understand their reticence until I traveled with the Zinacantec shaman Anselmo Perez to the United States. Anselmo had been invited to dedicate a Zinacantec house we had constructed in the main exhibit hall of the Science Museum of Minnesota. The opening festivities included a formal banquet. The dinner tables were set with a floral arrangement, candles, wine, and bread. As we sat down, Anselmo asked if this was a festival, and we told him it was, in a way. Then he asked, "Why do you have flowers on the table?" We answered, "Well, it's customary. We always do this." "Ah!" he said, "I knew you had forgotten."

Brocaded dogs and worms from Carranza; the "worms" also represent lightning

Anselmo pointed out that flowers, candles, bread, and wine are the essential elements of a Catholic altar—and a Maya festival. "There are flowers and candles because this is a celebration of Our Lord, and the bread and wine are a remembrance of his Last Supper. I knew you had forgotten the meaning of these things," said Anselmo smugly.

We rarely reflect upon the historical and symbolic significance of a banquet table or any of the other small rituals that permeate our lives. Likewise, Maya weavers simply take many of their myths for granted and fail to question the meaning of the symbols they weave every day.

Weavers are more concerned with creating something beautiful than describing it. They wear the clothes of the saints and have no doubt that their designs are vital and sacred. There are rules for the placement of designs in a *huipil*, but they are flexible, and a woman will alter the arrangement and create new harmonies within the boundaries of tradition. A weaver never repeats the same exact design twice: she will always make a little change, a slight variation in the form, size, and combinations of colors.

Each weaver will also focus attention on the mythical character she considers most important by making that motif more complicated or by including a number of variations of that design. The textiles of each community reflect its unique version of the myth of the Earthlord.

In Chenalhó the monster named Hairy Hand, represented by a row of spiky curls below the forest motif, appears on *huipiles*. According to myth, the Earthlord was picking fruit by the river that runs through Chenalhó when the monster Hairy Hand

grabbed him. Yusum saved the Earthlord by running to the Earthlord's cave, asking the toad Antonia to open the door, and bringing the Earthlord his drum. By playing his drum the Earthlord brought forth lightning and killed the monster.

117

Santa Cruz, from Chenalhó

Many figures on *huipiles* are called saints, even though they actually refer to the Earthlord. The designs for saints and toads resemble one another: weavers say, "A toad, a saint—it's all the same thing." In Magdalenas the larger design is called a saint and the smaller a toad, as if a saint were simply a toad that had grown up.

Saints or toads

Some symbols that appear on *huipiles* are part of neither the stories of the Flood nor the central myth of the Earthlord that appear as woven designs. A Holy Cross, woven with glowing points of color surrounding a small human figure, decorates the bottom edge of Chenalhó *huipiles*. This celebrates Santa Cruz, a miraculous apparition who descended from the sky over Chenalhó, and is honored in a chapel above the town where three crosses dressed in male ceremonial costume bestow their blessings on the people of the valley. The ceremonial *huipiles* of Tenejapa are almost identical to those of Chenalhó, as they were the models used by the three Chenalhó women at the turn of the century. There is no chapel to Santa Cruz in Tenejapa, however, so instead of a Holy Cross along the hem of the *huipil*, there is a toad. The women of Tenejapa originally learned how to brocade by studying the designs on a red-spotted toad.

Many designs—and the creatures of the underworld they represent—are interchangeable, just as the parts of the universe—the sky and the underworld—are mirror images of each other, infinite and reversible. On the sleeves of San Andrés *huipiles* are rows of small diamonds called "the wanderer," and sometimes along the edge of the design there is a crown. As the saints wander across the sky we see their crowns glowing as stars. The same diamonds may have small chevrons along the edge, which represent flowers and a field of corn. The designs for a star field and a cornfield are almost identical, for corn grows according to the seasons and the movement of the stars.

The *huipil* is a mirror of the universe and a portal to the Earthlord's cave. Toads surrounded by flowers wait on the border, the Earthlord stands amid snakes and thunderbolts, and the weaver, like the Earthlord's daughter, has prepared her cotton for dramatic transformation. The Earthlord may hesitate, but the weaver has placed among the flowers a scorpion to prod the lightning into creating rain clouds. The *huipil* is the woman's personal declaration that she has survived the evils that brought the Flood, has preserved the wisdom of the saints, and added life and color to their design. She is one woman, alone, who has prayed and cried and learned all by herself how to move the world.

Woven Clouds

There is a moment when heaven touches earth. Among the flowers and sprouting corn woven into a Magdalenas huipil, a toad dances in the rain. A Maya woman draws the clouds into her cloth, weaving the hidden forces behind the rains in designs to bring flashes of lightning overhead.

The first weavers, the saints, who still stand in Maya churches wearing the huipiles of their community, gave these woven designs to Maya women at the beginning of the world. A girl first prays to the saints for the skill and grace to weave and then learns the techniques from her mother, but to compose the ancient designs in a harmonious pattern that will move heaven and earth to bring the world to flower, a weaver dreams.

Sheep, first brought to the Highlands by the Spanish colonists, were called "cotton deer" by the Tzotzil Maya. The Spanish seemed equally confused: an early colonial drawing of a cotton plant shows a tiny sheep growing on top of a tall stalk.

Woolen garments became extremely valuable in the cool climate and quickly replaced the Pre-Columbian quilted-cotton garments of the past. Black sheep are especially prized for their fleece, as it can be easily dyed a lustrous coal black color with mud and herbs. Most Maya women had forgotten the art of dyeing fibers with leaves, barks, and berries until the Chiapas weavers' society, Sna Jolobil, experimented with dye plants and taught its members how to recreate the colors used by their ancestors.

ABOVE: A Zinacantec girl whirls a spindle weighted with a clay ball with one hand while she draws thread out of a combed tuft of wool with the other. Although it appears simple, spinning the yarn for a garment takes as long as weaving the cloth.

OPPOSITE: Unlike brocade, embroidered designs are made on finished cloth. The yoke of this Aguacatenango blouse is embroidered separately, then sewn onto the body of the garment.

BELOW: Brocaded designs similar to those seen on garments depicted in Classic Maya lintels are woven into cloth on the loom. An extra weft passes horizontally over and under warps to build up a design. The weaver, from San Andrés, uses a bone pick to lift the pile evenly.

ABOVE: Clothes are woven to size, not tailored from cut cloth; the length of the warp determines the length of the garment. Thread is stretched over and under rods tied to a warping board at the desired length. This girl from Zinacantan alternates groups of red and white threads in her warp to make a vertically striped cloth.

OPPOSITE: A backstrap loom is a flexible web. Warps that stretch up from these San Andrés weavers are held by rods tied at one end to a tree; the weaver can adjust the tension of the loom by leaning forward or back. The width of the warps tied to the rod sets the width of the finished cloth.

ABOVE: To weave a single line of cloth a weaver places a wooden batten, shaped like a thick, dull sword with blunt points at both ends, between the sets of warps, called sheds. The even-numbered warps form one shed and the odd warps the other. The batten is twisted on its side to form a narrow space between the sheds through which a shuttle, a thin rod wrapped with thread, is passed, leaving behind the line of thread called the weft.

OPPOSITE: To reverse the sheds for the next line a weaver uses a heddle, a rod that holds a string that loops under each odd warp. She leans forward and lifts up the heddle rod; all the odd warps are pulled up by the looped string of the heddle, but the even-warp shed stays in place. Again the batten is inserted in the space between the sheds to make room for the shuttle. Once the weft is in place it is pounded into a straight line with the batten.

OVERLEAF: With an extra weft a weaver can brocade the universe, mapping the four corners of the world. By connecting east, the diamond on top, and west, the diamond below, to the large central diamond she depicts the sun's path. The pair of curls on each side of the central diamond are the wings of a butterfly, woven as a metaphor for the sun's movement and the transformation from day to night.

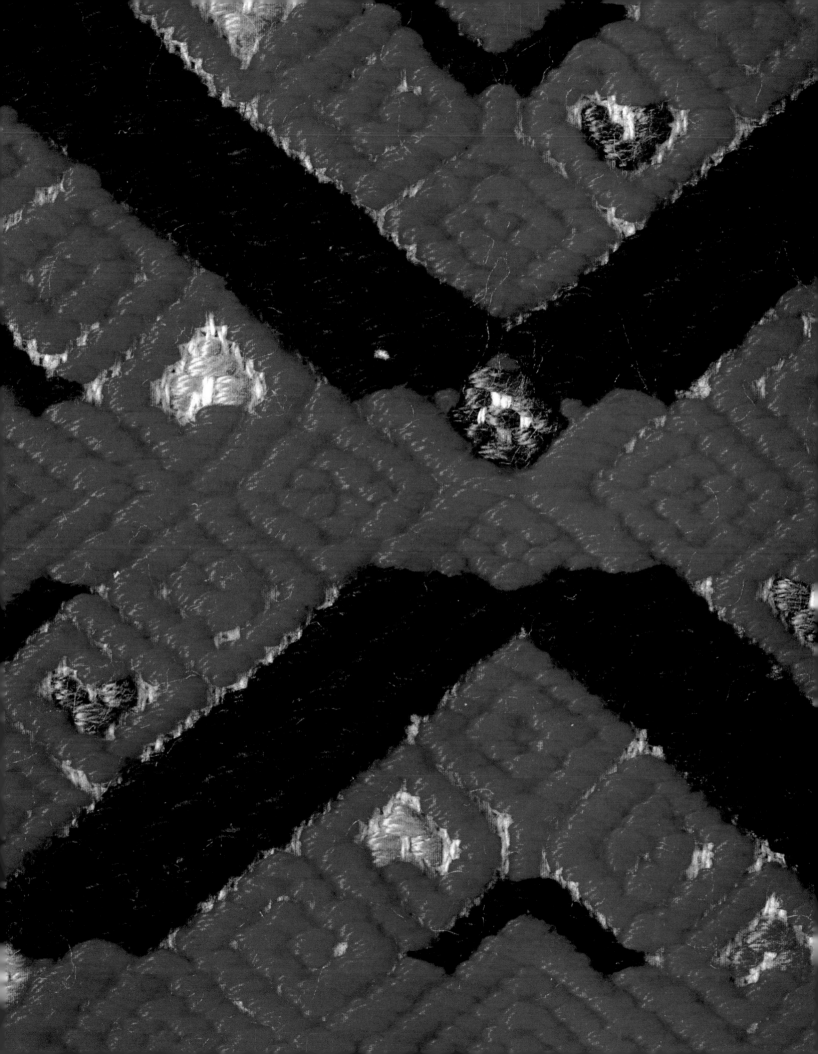

The warps that stretch before a weaver (opposite) are the matrix in which she places her brocade designs. The design is built up weft by weft as the dots of color woven into the gridwork slowly form a pattern. In a day a weaver may complete one inch of brocade.

In the loom above, the batten has pounded down a completed line of brocade. Under the shadow of her deer-bone pick can be seen the symbol of the weaver's community, Magdalenas—a vulture whose green head sits hunched between curled wings and the three lines of its body. Framed in yellow, the double red line of the next design represents mounds of earth piled over diamond-shaped seeds. Yet to be completed are the seeds' flowers, represented by the upside-down "V"s nested in the "X"s; the top half of each "X" will receive another "V" with two more lines of brocade, to create a symmetrical design that "flowers" in both directions.

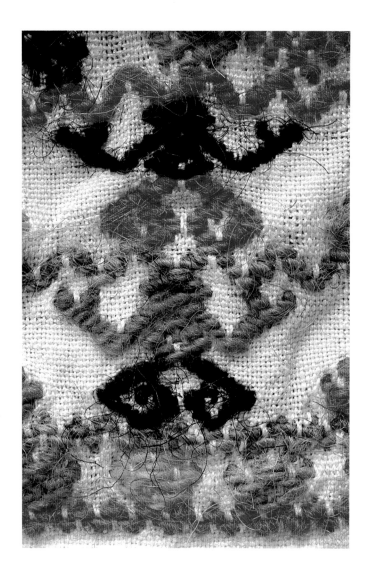 

Nichimal, or "flowery," is also the word for "beautiful" in Tzotzil Maya. A *huipil* describes the earth just as the first rains fall, a world in flower. The figures that dance with upraised hands along the edge of the brocade of the Magdalenas *huipil* (opposite) represent the Earthlord (detail above right) and his small assistant, the toad, who creates the rain clouds (detail above left). From his home in caves atop the mountain peaks, where clouds build every afternoon during the rainy season, the Earthlord transforms white cotton carded by his daughters into clouds with flashes of lightning. Toads are the Earthlord's musicians; their singing announces the coming of the rains.

On the *huipil* opposite the design below the toads is the weaver's personal signature. Within each community women can name the weaver of each textile by her individual style, but a quick glance at the signature pattern confirms her identity. Most weavers prefer to remain anonymous outside of their community, however; in deference to their wishes, these artists are not identified by name but by design. This woman is Lady Flowery Face of Our Father.

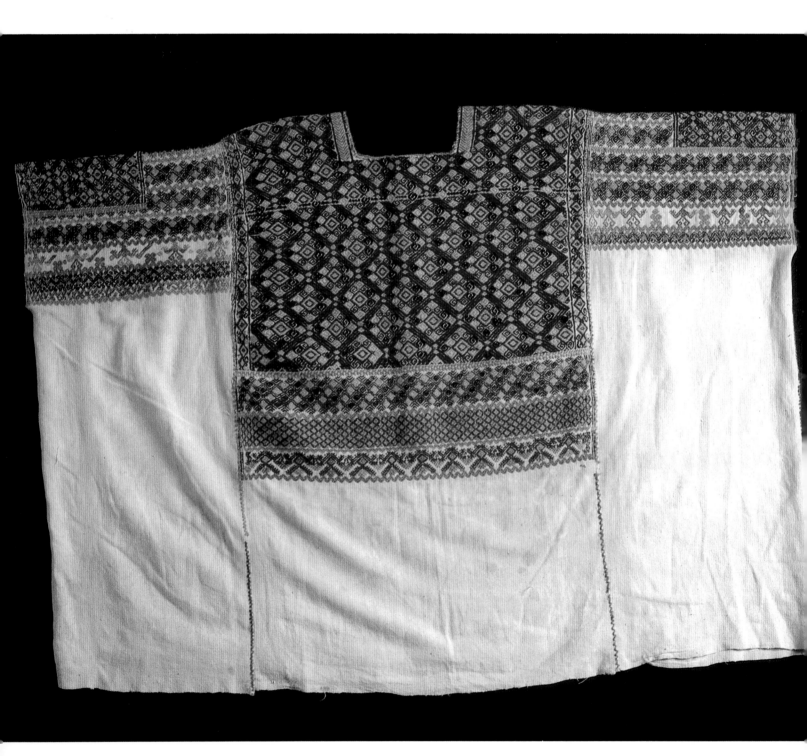

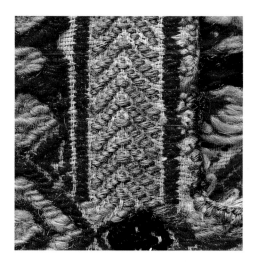 

A *huipil* encloses a woman in sacred space. Just as altars and crosses are ritually decorated with flowers and pine branches, the neck of the *huipil* opposite is encircled with a chevron design representing the flowering tip of pine (above left).

In the center of each dark diamond (above right), a curly-winged sun is shown in its daily motion along a narrow path from east, the small diamond above, to west, below. The sun's journey is repeated in fields that cover the bodice of the *huipil* and appear on the sleeves. When wearing her *huipil* the weaver is the center of the design of the world, which radiates in all four directions around her.

A row of Earthlords stands just above the white cotton weave of the bodice, and toads (below left) are framed in the white of the sleeves, along with the weaver's signature—Lady Toad's Back. Hidden among the flowers at the top of her sleeve is a scorpion (below right), which once bit the Earthlord's son Lightning Bolt; the scorpion is woven into the *huipil* to goad him into action. Like the daughters of the Earthlord in his mountain caves, the weaver has prepared her cotton for a flash of transformation into clouds.

 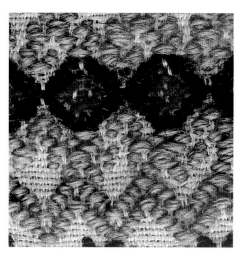

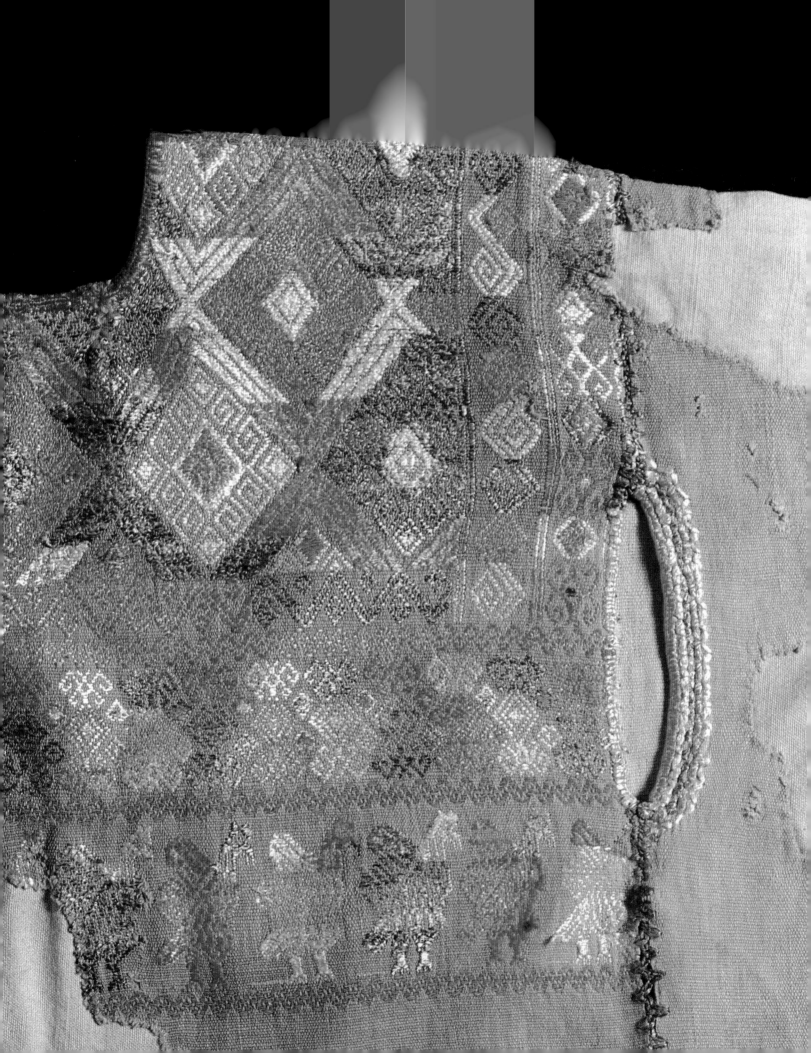

PRECEDING PAGES: The statue of Santa Rosario in Chamula wore this silk brocade *huipil* for more than a century. The head of the infant Jesus cradled in the Virgin's arms poked through the embroidered slit. When the *huipil* became too tattered for the saint to wear, church officials asked Rosha Hernandez of San Andrés to reproduce it, because Chamulas had lost the art of brocading in the nineteenth century. Rosha wove a new *huipil* for the saint and taught Chamula women how to brocade again.

ABOVE: The winners of the Magdalenas weaving contest in 1985 and three judges from San Andrés and Tenejapa line up for their portrait. A decade ago, before Sna Jolobil organized women in a dozen communities to revive traditional design, only five women in Magdalenas would have been able to weave the ceremonial *huipil*.

OPPOSITE: Judges of the weaving competitions are brought in from other communities to ensure impartiality. Rosha Hernandez, on the right, is Sna Jolobil's weaving teacher, and Micaea Hernandez Ruiz is the president of the San Andrés weavers. The husbands of the contestants add their own comments as the judges closely examine each piece, searching for flaws or for unusually fine execution of design. Women are encouraged to weave samplers such as this to perfect their work.

ABOVE: A brocaded design of Antonia, the toad who guards the entrance of the Earthlord's cave. Although a weaver's skill comes from divine inspiration, according to one legend brocade was first learned in Tenejapa when a woman saw a red-spotted toad in a cave and copied its pattern on her loom.

OPPOSITE: Lucia Gomez, the former president of Sna Jolobil, left, and her sister Petrona. Both master weavers, they are often given grants to study ceremonial constume. Supporting weavers is traditional in Tenejapa, where the community pays women to weave a set of clothes for Our Lady of the Lake. According to myth, the Virgin appeared in Lake Banabil and asked for a *huipil* and skirt so that she could dress as a proper woman. Each year the chosen weaver leads a procession of religious officials to the lake and throws the clothing into the water as an offering.

OVERLEAF, LEFT: Maria Tzu models the *huipil* that was awarded the national prize in 1980 as the best Mexican textile. Maria had spent two years studying the designs of an old Chamula *huipil* and learning how to dye yarns to match the original.

OVERLEAF, RIGHT: A strong person's soul is thought to be a jaguar, the lord of the animal spirits. This design from a San Andrés *huipil* shows a jaguar standing between green and yellow diamonds, with the tips of his upcurled paws spotted yellow and purple.

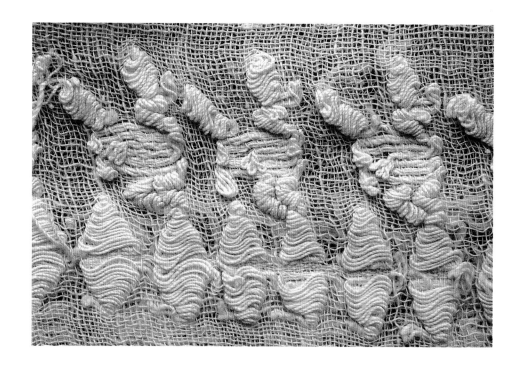

Although brocade motifs such as flowers, toads, jaguars, and the bird above, from Carranza, are of Pre-Columbian origin, a few European designs also appear in Chiapas textiles. Spanish nuns taught women cross-stitch embroidery patterns, and motifs such as the peacock below, from San Fernando, were adapted to brocade the turkey design opposite, from the Chamula *huipil* of Santa Rosario.

PRECEDING PAGES: Saint Martha, surrounded by ceremonial visitors from neighboring communities, is carried in procession around the plaza of Magdalenas. Around her neck hang mirrors and offerings of the first weavings made by young girls: before attempting the complex designs a young girl prays for the grace and skill to weave, and she dedicates her first work to the saint. Saints also wear layers of *huipiles* made by generations of weavers, thereby preserving the ancient designs.

THESE PAGES: Textiles are a fragile art. Weaving tradition, however, has proven stronger than stone. The *huipiles* of Magdalenas seen above have the same designs as those worn by Classic Maya royalty. The rulers' portraits lie in ruins abandoned more than a millennium ago, but weavers continued to wear the ancient designs and eventually wove them into the *huipiles* of the saints for future generations. Even subtle techniques such as this silken join of the *huipil* of Santa Rosario (opposite) remain for women to study and weave into their own garments.

The Ancestors' Dreams

Everybody may see a devil but only a few see God. The *Totil Me'il*, literally "Fathers-Mothers," also known as the Ancestors, reside in the mountains above each community and watch over the lives of their children. The Ancestors summon those with strong souls in their dreams to show them the proper and holy path of life and give them power over the jealous witches and demons that plague the night. People who ignore the Ancestors' teachings ignore the path that was laid down at the beginning of the world. Those with weak souls will grow ill.

The Ancestors represent the first people who learned how to plant corn, praise their creator, and live as proper human beings. Like the saints, they are not anyone's direct ancestors but supernatural beings who guard the entire community. The Ancestors and the saints are members of a family who meet to discuss the state of the world. God has empowered them both to intercede on behalf of mankind. The saints are the more remote group, for they are the stars that wander across the distant sky. The Ancestors dwell in the nearby mountains and hear more clearly their children's pleas for health and knowledge.

When men and women were first created, they could see everything, says the *Popol Vuh*. The creator gods thought this gave them too much power, and so "they were blinded as the face of a mirror is breathed upon. Their eyes were weakened. Now it was only when they looked nearby that things were clear." The ancestral gods restore some of that second sight in dreams. They summon men and women to serve as advocates for the sick, to plead for the restoration of a patient's soul before the holy judges. In dreams the Ancestors teach these chosen men and women how to cure a sick individual and how to maintain the well-being of the community. A person who can cure is known as *h'ilol*, "one who can see," for in dreams he or she has stood in the presence of the Ancestors. Bonesetters and midwives are taught their art in dreams, and musicians are shown how to play

OPPOSITE: Maria Meza of Tenejapa smiles at the awards ceremony of a weaving contest. Maria raised her son Pedro by herself, and he too became a weaver, which is unusual as weavers and potters are traditionally women in Chiapas. Such divisions along sexual lines are not written in stone, however: Classic Maya cities were ruled by women as well as men, religious office is shared by married couples, and the Ancestors call both men and women to serve as shamans.

San Andrés musicians

their instruments. Shamans journey in their dreams to the meeting place of the Ancestors to learn the flowers and herbs they must use and the prayers they must recite when curing patients. Sometimes the Ancestors will bless the whole community by sending revelations to a person wise enough to see.

One such person was Mol Comate, although nominally he was in charge of the musicians of Chenalhó. Every festival must have music, and, because it is a lifelong position, a musician often knows the rituals better than the men and women who act as patrons of each particular celebration. Musicians will prompt the religious officials if they have left out an important prayer and will guide the ritual to completion.

Fife and drum announce the procession of religious officials from one house to another, and fireworks punctuate their arrival. Harp, guitar, and violin play melodies derived from fifteenth-century chorals. The sound of strings is angelic. For three days and three nights the song of the festival rises and cries, unearthly, hypnotic. When the religious officials grow weary of dancing, when the cooks'

gossip becomes too barbed or a drunk has begun to wail his sins, the harp is still repeating with the guitar and violin the same melodies heard that morning and during every festival that has occurred on this day for each of the last 450 years.

As a musician Mol Comate maintained the community's traditions. But his true role was to announce the great visions that came to him in dreams. He was born in neighboring Chamula but came to Chenalhó in accordance with instructions he received in a dream. Although Maya rarely move from one community to another, the people of Chenalhó accepted the truth of his dream and welcomed him. When the Ancestors granted him a vision of the sacred world, he would proclaim his dream in the marketplace for all to hear. If the dream concerned the well-being of the community, the shamans of Chenalhó would gather to pray on the mountaintops for guidance. When Mol Comate saw a fiery cross descend from the heavens, settle on the Chapel of the Holy Cross on a hill above the town, then stand for a moment in front of the church, he knew that the cross was looking for a place to stay. The people rebuilt the chapel and dressed the wooden crosses standing on the altar in the finest Chenalhó costume.

What is most remarkable about Mol Comate's dream is that the same vision had occurred before in many Maya communities. In 1556 in Esquipulas, Guatemala, a vision of a black Christ descending on a fiery cross inspired the people to build a huge church that still attracts thousands of pilgrims to the site of the miracle. On the altar stands a gold cross, on which is hung a life-size sculpture of Christ carved in ebony. In Tila, Chiapas, the black Christ appeared at a Classic Maya shrine to Ek, the black god of the pole star and of merchants. The fiery cross recalls the World Tree, most clearly represented in Classic Maya sculptures at Palenque. In the Temple of the Foliated Cross the tree is shown growing out of the underworld and spreading out in all four directions, its top extending to the heavens.

In Chenalhó a flaming cross was seen descending from the heavens in 1711. That, together with the appearance of the Virgin Mary to a Maya girl in nearby Santa Marta, was taken as proof that Christ and the Virgin were Maya and would defend their people against the Spanish bishops and governors. Under the leadership of the girl from Santa Marta and a man from Chenalhó, an exclusively Maya church was organized, with its headquarters located in Cancuc. The Maya church slaughtered the Spaniards in outlying communities, but after a few initial successes the movement splintered and was crushed by troops brought in from Guatemala.

Dreams are powerful. Mol Comate's vision of the cross revived an ancient Maya symbol of the world. The cross, like the World Tree, is the path between the underworld and the heavens. Mol Comate led the people into honoring a sacred presence that, like ceremonial music, has deep spiritual reverberations. At the Chapel of the Holy Cross, or Santa Cruz, people pray for rains and a good harvest, the special providence of the Earthlord. Yet Santa Cruz is never im-

Flowering cross motif from Bochil

plored for evil purposes; it is known that Santa Cruz will relieve the humble in their suffering. The association of the fiery cross with violent rebellion and the malevolent powers of the Earthlord has been supplanted by Santa Cruz, which only helps those in need.

Mol Comate was a great dreamer.

The gift of sight is considered a burden that cannot be refused. If someone avoids accepting the Ancestors' summons, it is believed that his soul will no longer be cared for and he will die. A person's gift of sight is obvious to the whole community: if a shaman's patient does not recover, for example, he is denounced as not a shaman, but a charlatan; not "one who can see," but a "chicken eater" who conducts ceremonies only in order to eat the sacrificial chickens.

The powers of a shaman or curer are subtle and rarely lead to great wealth and prominence; he cures because that is his calling. A shaman is paid for his work and is given gifts of food, but, as his patients are seldom wealthy, a dedicated shaman may become impoverished by his vocation.

"My father was a shaman, and we had nothing to eat when I was a young girl," Rosha Hernandez of San Andrés once told me. Rosha is an extremely devout and knowledgeable woman who had served as a religious official, but she almost never summoned a shaman when she was sick. "It was terrible. My father was always off treating the neighbors. Sometimes he would bring back a little bit of chicken, but often there was nothing. My mother and I planted a little patch of potatoes, and that was all we had to live on. As a shaman my father had to drink during the ceremonies. When he came home he just slept. There was too much illness. He never had time to take care of the cornfield. Neighbors would come over to beg him to cure their families. He died when I was still a little girl."

Most shamans recognize the benefits of modern medicine and will prescribe pills as well as prayers. Mol Domingo of Chamula would examine his patient's pulse and press on various glands to diagnose the illness. He would offer prayers for a patient whose frightened pulse indicated that his soul had been stolen by witches, but if he thought it was some physical disorder caused by infection or parasites, he would send his patient to a doctor.

Most shamans insist that their role is to save the soul of the patient. Since shamans receive their knowledge in dreams, each one has a slightly different method of curing.

Ancestor design from San Andrés

Each Maya community interprets the powers of the Ancestors, saints, and Earthlord in a different manner. The Ancestors seen by a Zinacantec shaman are eighteen male and female personages who gather at Calvary mountain above Zinacantan center. There they decide when a soul created by God should be born or whether a person who is living immorally should be punished. The Maya of Zinacantan have an unusually logical set of beliefs and rituals associated with shamanism. Romin Tanchak explains the role and vision of "one who sees":

Whoever sees, dreams well.

Whoever becomes a shaman is summoned in their dreams to Calvary.

"We'll give you some work," the elders tell them. "Do you want to accept the responsibility of shamanhood, or don't you want to accept it?"

If they say, "I'll accept it," then it's fine. If they say, "I don't want to," they'll get a beating. They die.

If they do what they're told, they are given a little gourd for cooling flower water, the pot for their flowers, and their half-gourds for the ritual bath. They are given laurel, wintergreen, peperomia, and savory. They are given whatever medicines are needed to cure sickness. They are given the bamboo staff—the dog frightener.

After they receive their powers, they are eager to feel the pulse, they are eager to cure. In their dreams they are shown what to give for the illness.

The shaman sees the Ancestors sitting at a long table awaiting a ritual meal, just as the elders of Zinacantan sit at the Chapel of Esquipulas. The shamans offer candles and bowls of chicken soup.

If the elders eat right away, then the patient will recover right away.

If, on the other hand, the offerings aren't taken, the elders don't eat. "No, not yet," they say. "We'll see," they say.

If the elders watch over the patient, little by little he will recover. If they eat on the third day, he will still recover. But if they don't eat at all, the sickness won't pass.

He'll die at the first opportunity.

Midwives are also summoned in their dreams to Calvary, where they receive flowers and herbs. When bonesetters are called they are ordered to raise a fallen tree.

They pray over it! If they are able to set the big tree upright, then they will be successful setting bones. They acquire their powers that way. Even if our bone is badly broken, it will mend in three days.

Anselmo Perez, a Zinacantec shaman, agrees that his ability to heal comes from dreams. Parts of the ceremony, certain ways of arranging the flowers, and phrases used in his prayers were learned from observing shamans as a child, but Anselmo was taught to cure when the Ancestors summoned him to their table in the meeting place at Calvary.

Dreams are often shared. Shamans meet together and eat a ritual meal in their dreams. A person who falsely claims to be a curer will soon be discovered, as the deceiver will not be present at the dream meeting. That one is not a true seer but a witch who sells the souls of his enemies to the Earthlord.

The Earthlord, from San Andrés

Witches persuade the Earthlord to buy a soul with offerings of candles and prayers at mountain caves, the entrance to his underworld domain. When a per-

Drawing from a Tenejapan story of a priest who thought a falling comet would lead him to riches

son's soul is sold he works as a slave, gathering dried bones for firewood or tending the Earthlord's herds of deer. If a shaman cannot rescue the person's soul his patient will die.

"When you get sick, the witch may offer to help you, for a fee, and go to the caves again to buy back your soul. A nasty business," Anselmo explains. A Zinacantec who prays alone at the mouth of a cave is there to sell a soul. Anselmo would never go to a cave except in the company of other shamans during a public prayer for rain. If one of his patients was suffering from witchcraft, he would light small candles to "close the eyes" of the witch and the Earthlord, then pray with large candles to the Ancestors so that they might intercede with the saints and God to return the soul.

Weavers and shamans in other communities see the Earthlord as an ambivalent character, but Zinacantec shamans consider him to be basically evil and believe that God, the saints, and the Ancestors will overcome the Earthlord and thwart witchcraft—and save a man's soul.

Shamanism, in Anselmo's eyes, is a Christian activity. A shaman takes his patient's case before the Ancestors and defends him "like a lawyer," as Anselmo says. It is the shaman's ability to see and know the Ancestors in his dreams, as well as his gift of flowery speech, that will eventually convince the holy gathering to intercede on behalf of his patient. There is no magic involved, unless one is dealing with the

Drawing from a story of how Zinacantec elders defeated the demons in Guatemala.
The designs above their heads represent their animal spirits

Earthlord. "The soul was made by God, and he, not the Earthlord, is its rightful owner. God will retrieve my patient's soul from the Earthlord."

God, to the Maya, is the Father, the Son, and the Holy Ghost, the mystical Trinity the Maya accepted in the sixteenth century. The word for "us" in Tzotzil and Tzeltal Maya is *kristianoetik*, which literally means "we Christians." Maya Christianity has retained the teachings, rituals, and medieval flavor of Spanish Catholicism, including a belief in the devil and witchcraft.

"Who knows why someone becomes a witch, an *ak'chamel*, a giver of illness?" says Anselmo. "Perhaps they just like to feel powerful." Witches are beyond the social norms, perverse creatures who transform themselves into wild beasts, corpse eaters, or charcoal crunchers, and, as the following story relates, they can appear suddenly and with no warning:

There was a man sleeping with his wife.
She was a Charcoal Cruncher.
The man touched his wife in the dark. Just the stump of her was there. She had no head.
He lit a match. "Where did my wife go?" he said. "How could it be? Could someone have cut off her head?
"Who knows? There must be a reason. Maybe she took a walk. Maybe she's bad. I guess I'll see if she's a devil."
He put salt on the stump of her neck.

When the woman's head rolled home from crunching coals, it wouldn't stick to the rest of her. Her head was flopping about like a chicken. It bounced and bounced.
And she died.

Witchcraft is the cause of many ills. If someone slips and falls on a mountain path, it is thought that a witch has asked the Earthlord to separate parts of that person's soul from the body. A shaman quickly arrives to gather up the lost pieces of the soul before nightfall, when a witch may come to claim the soul.

Every person's soul has thirteen parts. A fall or an act of witchcraft can cause a person to lose a few parts and become debilitated and sick. Fright can also loosen a person's soul from his body, as the soul is always trying to free itself and return to heaven, from whence it came. When the first airplane flew over Zinacantan in the 1950s, shamans were busy for weeks patching people together again.

Each person also has a companion animal spirit, which lives in a corral inside the mountains and is fed and protected by the Ancestors. In dreams a person may see or become his animal spirit. The animal often reflects the personality of the individual. The humble may be deer and the licentious squirrels, since squirrels fornicate in the treetops where everyone can see. A powerful shaman may have more than one animal spirit, including the jaguar, lord of the holy animals; shamans and witchs have the power to transform themselves into their animal spirits.

A witch's companion animal spirit is a wild bird that is not cared for by the Ancestors, often an owl. Their screeches at night are always a bad omen.

If the Ancestors observe that a person is behaving badly and has not paid attention to their warnings, they will let that person's animal spirit out of the corral and into the world. If the animal gets injured, so will the person; if it is shot and killed by hunters, then, unless he has more than one animal spirit, the person will die.

If someone is sick he asks a shaman to examine him. A shaman first feels the pulse of his patient by putting his fingers on the patient's wrist. He listens to the movement of the blood to discover a tremor that will indicate whether the patient's soul has been sold to the Earthlord or his companion animal spirit is wandering loose in the mountains. The curing ceremony differs in each community.

According to Anselmo, if a Zinacantec shaman determines that the illness has been caused by displeasing the Ancestors, he asks the family to find four men to gather holy flowers and water and four women to prepare a ritual meal. The shaman will return to plead the patient's case when all is ready.

The male assistants bring a gourd of water from each of the seven holy springs in Zinacantan that were "given by Our Lord to cure sickness." They go to the woods to gather the tips of pine branches, flowers of air plants, myrtle and laurel leaves, geranium flowers, and sticks of the copal tree. One assistant will go to the market to buy the boiled resin of copal for incense, black chickens, and liters of *posh*—sugarcane liquor.

At dusk the shaman arrives at the courtyard of the patient's house; he carries with him his bamboo staff of office, which also serves to ward off the dogs yapping in the yard. First he blesses himself before the cross that stands in front of each house, facing the setting sun. Making the sign of the cross four times over his forehead, eyes, mouth, and heart, he seals the house from any evil intrusions.

A Tenejapan shaman pouring posh *into a drinking gourd. The patient is incensed and brushed with flowering branches as part of the cure*

When the shaman comes in he finds the patient lying on a bed of pine needles and flowers. He bows to the elders in the family and touches the foreheads of the youths and those serving as his assistants. A palm mat holding the leaves, branches, and flowers is unrolled next to a table covered with a ceremonial cloth. An incense burner and a bottle of *posh* stand ready as the shaman counts the flowers.

Three of each kind of flower, three pine branches, and three sticks of incense are mixed with a handful of myrtle and laurel leaves and carefully arranged in a clay pot. Water from the seven holy springs is added, and the pot is placed on the open fire. The mixture of that which is beautiful, strong, and alive is steeped into a "flower water" to bathe the patient.

The female assistants have already killed one chicken, hung it upside down to drain the blood, and plucked the feathers. Sometimes the chicken is cut into thirteen parts to correspond to the patient's soul, but since Anselmo never saw the need for this in his dreams, the chicken used in his curing ceremony is cut into bite-sized pieces and boiled. Chicken soup is an essential ingredient in a curing ceremony.

Coffee mixed with lumps of brown sugar is also served. A special drink of corn gruel boiled with unrefined sugar until it thickens like pudding may also be prepared for the patient. *Ul*, as it is called, is described in ritual speech as being like the rains, like the semen of the gods.

Before the meal is served the shaman arranges on the table the flowers that will be carried to the mountain shrines of the Ancestors. The candles that will be burnt in offering are counted, laid out, and decorated with flowers. Then the youngest male assistant opens a bottle of *posh* and pours out shots for each member of the family, each ritual assistant, and the shaman. The shot glass is an offertory candle holder with a cross etched on the side. There is only one glass, so each person must either toss the liquor down quickly or touch his lips to the *posh* and pour the rest into a bottle to drink later. The cup bearer pours three quick rounds. When the assistants receive the glass the shaman touches their foreheads, names them as helpers, and reminds them of the role they play.

A shot of *posh* may be a blessing on a cold winter's night, but by the time the cup bearer brings the ninth round the gift has become a burden. The participants in a curing ceremony consume *posh* for the same reason they burn candles—it is a gift for the saints and Ancestors. *Posh* is considered a powerful healing substance and also a cause of sickness, for the hangovers are unbearable. Everyone who drinks offers the spirit of all that is joyous and terrible in life.

Next the shaman blesses the candles that will be offered at the shrines on seven holy mountains. On the last, Calvary, the patient is finally presented before the Ancestors. A Zinacantec prayer describes the pilgrimage that will restore the patient's soul:

K'usi ti nopbile,
  K'usi ti p'isbile,
K'usi yepal 'un, jtot?
  K'usi yepal 'un, kajval?
Ch'ul-tzoblebal,
  Ch'ul-lotlebal,
Tzoblebal 'avalab,
  Tzoblebal 'anich'nab,
Tzoblebal ch'ul-totil
  Tzoblebal ch'ul-me'il.

What has been decided,
  What has been weighed?
How much, My Father
  How much, My Lord?
Holy gathering place,
  Holy meeting place,
Gathering place of thy Child,
  Gathering place of thy offspring,
Gathering place of the Holy Fathers,
  Gathering place of the Holy Mothers.

Take heed, My Father,
  Take heed, My Lord!
So he begs holy pardon,
  So he begs divine forgiveness,
For one moment,
  For two moments,
He goes kneeling,
  He goes bowed low,
To thy thresholds,
  To thy altars,
He goes to weep,
  He goes to shout,
With his spouse,
  With his companion.
So he goes offering a splinter of his lowly torch,
  So he goes offering a shaving of his humble
    candle,
However anxious his heart,
  However vexed his heart,
With his spouse,
  With his companion,
Holy Father,
  Holy Mother,
Place of gathering,
  Place of meeting,
Take heed, My Father,
  Take heed, My Lord!
What now shall be decided,
  What now shall be weighed?
For one moment,

For two moments,
We go walking,
  We go stepping,
To thy threshold,
  To thy altar,
I speak,
  I converse,
Before thy beauteous lordly face,
  Before thy beauteous lordly eyes,
I suffer my pains,
  I endure my hardship,
Take heed, My Father,
  Take heed, My Lord:
May it be accepted,
  May it be received.
The sum of my lowly mouth,
  The sum of my humble lips,
Calvary, My Father,
  Calvary, My Lord.

Before the climb to the mountain shrines, the patient is bathed in flower water and his clothes are censed with copal. While he is being cleansed, the people gathered round the patient drink three more rounds of *posh*.

One black chicken is brought forward and washed in the flower water. Again three rounds of *posh* are shared. This chicken is offered in exchange for the patient's soul, to balance its return to the surface of the earth. Some shamans leave the chicken in a niche under the shrine at Calvary. Anselmo feels that this is unnecessary, as those that are spirit can eat only spiritual food. Anselmo will know from the patient's pulse whether the Ancestors have accepted the chicken, a sign they will restore his patient's soul.

The ritual assistants cross themselves as they place the candles in a net bag, then sit down for a fortifying meal of tortillas and chicken soup that has been brewing on the fire. The women stay next to the fire, demurely passing heated tortillas to the men and picking at the food.

Tenejapan shaman praying before the house cross

Once they have eaten, the shaman and his male assistants cross themselves again as they prepare to leave for "Holy Heaven" on the mountaintops. The shaman bows to the elder female assistants, who touch his forehead; he in turn touches the foreheads of the younger women. Striding outside with his bamboo staff, the shaman blesses himself before the house cross. His assistants, who carry the candles, flowers, and *posh*, do the same. Then the party leads the patient, if he is well enough to walk, on the hard trek to the shrines.

The sacred mountains stand like steep pyramids around Zinacantan center. At the base and top of each mountain are several wooden crosses set in stone and concrete, with a small pit in front to shield candles from the wind. The shaman presents his patient at each mountain shrine, addressing all the saints and Ancestors in his prayers in the hope that one will take up his cause as they gather in judgment in the night. Three branches of geranium flowers are tied at the center, the heart, of the crosses there. When the shaman decorates the crosses with flowers, he opens the portal to the sacred world. The Ancestors measure his grace and humility as he lights the candles and prays for his patient's soul.

The shaman, confident that his acts and prayers have convinced at least one of the saints or Ancestors that his patient deserves to live, brings the patient back to his home, where the two kneel before the house cross. The old flowers are removed and replaced with flowers that were carried to the mountaintops. Candles that also made the journey are lit while the shaman prays for his patient's soul to return home.

The patient is brought inside, where he is finally allowed to rest on a soft bed of palm mats, wool blankets, and sweet-smelling pine needles. A pillow made of flowers from the shrines is laid under his head to direct the return of his soul.

To learn what has been decided at the meeting of the Ancestors, the shaman places thirteen kernels of each of the four colors of corn—black, yellow, red, and white—and a little salt from a mountain spring in a bowl of water next to the patient's head. The kernels that float indicate how many of the thirteen parts of the soul are still adrift.

The patient stays in bed for three days, during which time the house is closed to visitors. When the shaman returns on the third day, he feels the pulse of his patient to listen for the sounds of a lost soul. If the patient's companion animal spirit is still missing in the mountains, the shaman prepares to argue his case again in an even more elaborate ceremony. If the blood is quiet and regular, he knows that the Ancestors have returned the patient's animal to the safety of the corral in the heart of the mountain.

When the shaman is satisfied that his patient's soul is well cared for, he removes the pine needles and flower pillow from the bed. These will be carried to San Kristoval hill and returned to the Ancestors.

As the shaman departs, he salutes the head of the household:

My Father,
  My Lord?
Thanks to you all,
  May God repay you.
You measure me as a man,
  You measure me as a person.
The words are over,
  The lips are still,

We have finished begging holy pardon,
  We have finished begging divine forgiveness,
My Father,
  My Lord.
My earth will go on,
  My mud will go on.
Now we have begged holy pardon,
  Now we have begged divine forgiveness.
At the thresholds,
  At the altars,
Of the Holy Fathers,
  The Holy Mothers,
May there not yet arise,
  May there not yet pass,
The seeming good,
  The evil,
At my lowly back,
  At my lowly side,
Thanks to you all, then, my Father,
  My Lord,
Thanks to you all.

Of course shamanism works. For three days the entire family's attention has been focused on the well-being of its sick member, as the shaman has choreographed their movements into a harmony of flowers, prayers, and sacrifices. The ritual assistants, who normally are also members of the family, share their relative's struggle. The Ancestors, the Fathers-Mothers of all Zinacantecs, gather at Calvary to restore one of their children to health. The patient's soul and his will to live are revived through rituals that confirm he is a valued member of his family and his community.

Illness is thought to be caused by the envy of witches or by the patient's own lack of respect for the proper ways of behavior. The patient is led along the flowering path of well-being by the shaman, who has made the patient's family and the Ancestors allies in his struggle to live righteously. He is no longer an outcast; like his companion animal spirit, he is cared for and nurtured at home. Together the shaman and relatives have convinced the saints and Ancestors to reclaim his soul from the Earthlord.

Sometimes a shaman must address the Earthlord directly. One such occasion is when a new house is built. Since the building sits on the earth, the Earthlord must be paid.

When the roof beams of a new house are in place and the walls are completed, but before the house is roofed over with thatch or tile, a chicken is hung by a rope from a central beam. A square pit is dug in the center of the floor and the chicken's throat is slit so that the blood drips into the hole. Then the chicken is placed in the earth and the pit is filled and tamped down. The Earthlord, having been compensated for the use of the land and the trees cut into roof beams, will not claim the owner's soul. On the spot where the chicken was buried are put the three hearthstones of the house.

The shaman is not summoned until the house is finished. The cross that leans against the west wall of every Maya house is decorated with flowers. The shaman prays before the cross, burning candles and incense in benediction of the new home. A ritual meal of chicken soup is prepared, and the shaman pours a little soup in the four corners of the house and in the center, while the cup bearer serves three rounds of *posh* each time the shaman blesses a new direction.

The house must be fed, lest it eat its inhabitants. The beams that had been cut from the forest must be blessed, lest the forest claim the owner's souls in exchange for the felled trees. The shaman cures the house, much as he cures a sick patient, leading it through prayer to the proper way of being. The house is kept shut for three days while it recovers.

When there is a drought the shamans, as a group, may address the Earthlord directly. No one doubts that the shamans who leave the community center in procession will plead only that the Earthlord release the clouds he creates. Witches work alone.

On the third of May, the shamans from the cere-monial centers, hamlets, and settlements who share the same spring gather together to pray, play music, and celebrate the existence of each miraculous source of water. A spring that continues giving clean water all year long is a constant surprise that deserves respect.

The festival of the Holy Cross, Santa Cruz, marks the beginning of the rains. The water holes are cleaned out, the crosses are renewed with flowers, and the musicians play to the water to keep it happy. All the people who use the spring help in the cleaning and decoration. The shamans among them pray to the saints and Ancestors to preserve this gift. They then enter the mountain caves to offer flowers, candles, incense, fireworks, and chickens as payment to the Earthlord. Directing the waters is an act of the Earthlord that benefits mankind. Zinacantec shamans honor the Earthlord at the beginning and the end of the rainy season.

Like the Chapel of Santa Cruz that was made from dreams in Chenalhó, the festival at Santa Cruz focuses the community's attention on the good that flows from the earth and its Lord. The neighbors who have been quarreling all year, the destitute and the wealthy, the witches who play with evil, and the shamans who strive for well-being must all come to the well for their water. They put on a display of unity before the one element that they all depend on. Santa Cruz is a celebration of neighborhoods and community, a spring fest that promises renewal and a remembrance of the daily needs that bind people together.

On festival day the cross that guards the spring is opened, like a gate against evil, by decorating it with pine boughs and flowers, so that the Earthlord and all the powers may see the good works of man. The Ancestors can see that the community lives as it should, and the celebration reassures God that his creation is honored and enjoyed.

These celebrations negate the sins that could cause the world's destruction. God has destroyed the

Prayers before the statue of Saint John the Baptist, the patron saint of Chamula

world at least once with a flood, and would like to try his hand at creation once again. He remains distant, like an emperor in a heavenly court, concerned about his people but unwilling to worry about all the details. The Ancestors of each community are empowered to judge their people, whom they know intimately. The Lords of each mountain, the Lords of the Earth, maintain the wild animals, flowers, and vegetation. A person may bribe them through witchcraft to bring untimely death upon a neighbor. God abhors this evil, and wonders if it is time to start anew.

God tried to destroy the world in 1983. A small volcano in northeastern Chiapas, named *El Chichonal*, "the nipple," blasted out more ash than the eruption of Mount Saint Helen. The Zoque villages near the volcano were buried as houses and churches collapsed under the weight of the ash. Their world ended that day.

Soon after, a dark cloud rolled over the Highlands. The sun disappeared for two days. White ash fell silently, hot and dry, like a snowstorm from another world. The air was too heavy for birds to fly; they fluttered in confusion on the ground, and the cats feasted.

Everything was white. The world had no color until a rainstorm swept in and washed away some of the ash. Juan de la Cruz Uchum'o, a friend from Chamula, came by my house ten days after the ash fell to ask me to contribute to the ceremonies in Chamula.

"Each family is paying for candles, incense, and sky rockets that are being offered at each spring, at every holy lake, at the mountaintops and caves," said Juan.

"Do you hope to stop the volcano?" I asked.

"Oh no, if God has decided to destroy the world, then he will. We can't change that. No, we are just asking the Earthlord for a little rain to clean off the ash."

"Will it work?"

"It rained last week, didn't it? That's because we prayed, and now we are asking for a little more."

During the next year the gray shroud of ash was cleansed from each statue, one by one, on that saint's feast day. The saints were then carried in procession outside the church, as they are even in uneventful years, to bear witness that the Maya are faithfully continuing the festivals in their honor and remain happy on this earth. Without these periodic confirmations of the rightness of the world, God would send from the heavens a rain of fire to cleanse the world and make way for a new creation. The Ancestors impart wisdom in dreams, and the Earthlord sends life-giving rains, but it is only through the festivals of the saints that the Maya can influence God, who controls the destiny of the world.

The Saints' Day

In Mol Sanate's house, where I lived in San Andrés, nothing happened on Christmas. There were no presents, there was no celebration; in fact, no one even mentioned Christmas. In the granary where I slept there was a small, neglected altar with a picture of the Virgin above a few clay candleholders and incense burners. In the middle of the night, the grandmother of the house came into the granary and lit a candle at the shrine. I woke up and asked her why. "Don't you know?" she asked. "It's Christmas."

Christmas, like all Maya holy days, is not celebrated at home but in the church. The responsibility for taking care of the saints, praying, and offering candles and devotion is assumed by married couples from the community. Each saint, Virgin, and Christ in the church is served for a year by these religious officials, whose duties culminate on the saint's day. Young couples who prepare the small festivals for less important saints are addressed as *Martoma*. Once they have mastered ritual speech and earned the respect of the community, they take on the financial burden of preparing, now as *Alféreces*, the main festival for the patron saint of the community. Under the guidance of an elder ritual advisor the couple organize the cooks and musicians and buy the candles, incense, fireworks, *posh*, and food necessary to honor the saints. The personal sacrifice of the religious officials sustains the community.

On Christmas Eve in Mitontik the church is heavy with incense. Musicians play before the altar, where, under a canopy of tropical fruits, orchids, and Spanish moss, there rests a small crèche. Baby Jesus and his brothers lie in the manger as Mary, Joseph, the Three Kings, and Maya shepherds look on. In the corner, religious officials prepare tortillas for the Christ Child and the Holy Family. All evening the townspeople stream in to worship at the crèche and stay to eat and drink with the religious and civil officeholders. At midnight the municipal president's wife holds the statue of Baby Jesus and carries it around the church as the people sing. She and her husband have adopted Jesus as their own child in the name of the whole community, which has become his family.

In the church in Zinacantan there is a grand procession led by two young boys dressed as angels in tall, red crowns, green velvet frock coats, and breeches. Behind these "angels" are two young men playing turtle-shell drums; these in turn are followed by bands of harpists, guitarists, and violinists and finally by the sacristans, religious officals, scribes, and elders. The spiritual leaders parade past the crèche and out to the plaza, where the main festivities are held.

In front of the crosses above the church a comic burlesque is performed by two men dressed as "Grandfathers" in wool shirts and red masks and two men dressed as "Grandmothers" in shabby skirts and *huipiles*. The Grandparents are mock representations of the Ancestors. Through their clumsy, bawdy actions, they reveal to every child and adult who sees their antics the consequences of improper behavior. They lead a bull made of palm mats, which they announce was bought in the lowlands at a ridiculously high price. The Grandfathers gallop about on "horses"—hobby horses made of carved and painted wood—and attack the bull as if they were toreros. But they immediately fall over, wailing that the bull gored them and broke their bones. The Grandmothers rush over in great alarm, push the sticks between their husbands' legs, and try to lift the Grandfathers by the crotch, which only adds to the injury. Next the Grandfathers are brought to the nearest religious official. Reciting the words of the bonesetter's prayer with some small modifications, the elder strokes each man's crotch with a feathered rattle, trying to set the bone straight, make it rise, make it firm:

Find your place, bones!
Find your place, muscles!
Don't leave your hole, muscle!
Don't leave your hole, bone!

The Grandfathers are miraculously cured and jump up to ride again.

The Grandmothers also try to ride horses, but, since Maya women never ride, they too fall off and must have their bones mended. Once cured, the Grandmothers attempt to teach the women in the audience how to spin, reminding them of their proper role in society and admonishing them to weave and work hard for their husbands. Meanwhile, someone notices that the Grandparents have no receipt for the bull they say they purchased; they are quickly arrested. The Grandfathers huddle by the jail door while the Grandmothers weep outside, begging the municipal president to release their husbands, who they say are simply fools. The Grandfathers, revealed as braggards and thieves, are finally released to perform with the Grandmothers this farce again, an example to the people of the sins that should be left behind in the coming year.

For the Maya, New Year's is a solemn celebration, for the world ends and is renewed with each new cycle. Candles illuminate the church in Chamula on New Year's Eve. The high ceiling, blackened by years of burning incense, absorbs the flickering light and the chants of shamans. On this night, as they kneel before the saints or stand in the center of the church before rows of candles, the shamans recite the prayers of a curing ceremony not for a patient who has lost his soul but for the well-being of the world.

In the municipal building fresh pine boughs are tied to the wooden crosses as a sign of new life. As the new officials are sworn in, the judges, councilmen, and municipal president sing prayers and dance to the timeless rhythm of harp and guitar. The change of office for civil officials occurs during the New Year's ceremony in January or at the start of the fiscal year in June.

Religious officials who serve the saints follow a sacred calendar that begins and ends on the saint's day. On the eve of the saint's day a wooden box wrapped in mats is carried to the house of the current religious official, where it is opened in the presence of the new *Martoma*. Inside the box are ancient fragments of the saint's clothing and stubs of candles that represent the many offerings made by the *Martoma* during the previous year. By counting the candles the husband acknowledges the responsibility that he and his wife share—to perform the ceremonies that will demonstrate to God that mankind remains faithful and happy on this earth. The saint's clothing represents the continuity of tradition from the beginning of the world; the Maya believe that the world will end unless these teachings from its beginning are preserved. The new *Martoma* repacks the box and brings the symbols of the past and the signs of his future devotions to his home. As he walks along the trail bearing the wrapped box with a tumpline, he reenacts a scene in Classic Maya hieroglyphic texts in which the days, months, and years are depicted as a burden carried with a tumpline on the back of a human figure. Religious officials are year bearers, carrying the world forward to the next cycle.

Within these endlessly repeating cycles the world changes. During the festival of San Sebastian in Zinacantan the beliefs and history that shaped the community are acted out by pairs of outgoing religious officials, who assume the roles of supernatural beings, such as the Earthlord and the old gods who bring rain and corn, along with the evil spooks, wild animals, savages, and immoral Spaniards who were overcome by the Zinacantecs. Like the lewd pantomimes of the Grandparents at Christmas, the rowdiness of the festival of San Sebastian encourages proper behavior through ridicule of its opposite. The festival is brilliant theater—raucous, spirited, and cathartic.

Mossmen wear strands of Spanish moss streaming from their wide black hats to their knees. Shrouded in the thick, gray moss, the two men dance like moving haystacks. Their costume alludes to Moss Mountain, the sacred mountain of Chamula that is the principal abode of the Earthlord.

A Chamula Martoma *incensing the saint's coffer*

The ancient gods, whose names have not been spoken for centuries, also appear in disguise. The Whiteheads wear trilobe masks that are attibuted to Tlaloc, the rain god for most of the ancient peoples of Mexico and Central America. The Whiteheads, with white sisal fiber on their hats, also imitate the gray-haired Ancestors of Zinacantan.

Mossmen and Whiteheads appear in the festival as witnesses to the celebration of historic victories and the arrival of the patron saints. Saint Sebastian is an early Christian martyr, a Roman soldier executed by archers after his conversion. Before the conquest, Maya captives were sacrificed in a similar manner. The statues brought by Spanish missionaries, showing Saint Sebastian pierced by arrows, were familiar and tragic icons to the Maya.

In Zinacantan, Saint Sebastian is said to be a Spanish soldier who was pursued by the Chiapanecs and devils and eventually arrived in Zinacantan. Tonik Nibak's story of the arrival of Saint Sebastian in Zinacantan includes most of the characters who appear in the festival.

The Holy Martyr, Saint Sebastian, was a captain. He came from deep in the woods with his little slit drum.

The slit drum, a hollowed log with an H-shaped slit on the top to form two vibrating tongs, is a Pre-Columbian instrument, associated with Votan, a post-Classic ruler of Chiapas, who was also called the Lord of the Hollow Trunk. For the festival of San Sebastian, an ancient slit drum is carried on a tumpline by one of the assistants while a musician hits the drum with a stick, playing a simple rhythm. The *tun, tun, tun* sound of the drum is also the ancient Maya word for year. A pictograph of a slit drum appears in hieroglyphic texts preceding the year bearers.

I don't know what Our Holy Father's crime was. They left him in the heavy forest to be killed by mountain lions, coyotes, jaguars. They did their best where they threw him. They tried their hardest where they tossed him, but he didn't die. He returned.

"How can it be that he doesn't die? We thought he would be killed by coyotes. We thought he would be eaten by jaguars, by some wild animal in the woods, but he returned just the same, alive."

Jaguars were once so numerous, according to the myths, that they threatened human existence. They were finally trapped on stone benches by an ancient hero who let one pair survive. During the festival, "Jaguars" dance on a boulder and are ritually trapped and let loose.

The jaguar impersonators wear baggy cotton suits painted with jaguar spots and a jaguarskin pillbox hat with a tail hanging down the back. Aztec codices show warriors dressed in similar jaguar suits holding lances tipped with obsidian blades. The Zinacantecs successfully fought off Aztec incursions into the Highlands in the fifteenth century.

The Lacandons were sent to shoot him [Saint Sebastian] with arrows. He was wounded in his breast. He was wounded in his legs. He was wounded in the belly, in his thighs, in his ribs. They tried to kill him because he was an army captain. How would we know he was Our Holy Father the Martyr? He looked like the image of Our Holy Father the Martyr in the church.

The Lacandon in the festival is called Cabinal, the name of Lacandon chiefs who fought the Zinacantecs when they joined the Spanish troops in their attempt to subdue the last Maya holdouts in Chiapas in the sixteenth century. The few hundred Lacandons living in the distant rain forest are still regarded as wild savages. Cabinal dances around in a long, blue wool *huipil*, carrying a little wooden bow with which he pretends to shoot people.

Raven came. The Spooks came with their squirrels.

Raven was mankind's benefactor after the Flood; it was he who first brought corn to man. He is played by a pair of outgoing religious officials, who wear wooden wings and conical hats with long beaks that hold an ear of corn. Raven is called K'uk'ulchan, "the Feathered Serpent" in Tzotzil. Quetzalcoatl, the

Feathered Serpent, was the mythical divine king of the Toltecs; his reign is remembered as a time of peace and abundant harvests. As a god he is associated with wind and rain and is pictured in Pre-Columbian codicies as wearing a beaked conical hat similar to the one worn by Raven.

The Spooks, who stalk the countryside and kidnap women, are played by local policemen wearing black clothes and masks. They carry stuffed squirrels, weasels, monkeys, and jaguarundis. The Spooks climb a tall, denuded tree set up in the field near the Church of San Sebastian; the tree sways precariously as they throw the stuffed animals at the spectators, shouting obscene jokes and accusations.

And then the Spaniards came.

It was the Spaniards who defended him long ago. "Don't kill him. He is our captain," said the Spaniards. "He will come to live here in the church."

The Spanish Gentlemen in the festival bear no resemblance to the early friars who brought Saint Sebastian to Zinacantan and briefly defended the Maya against colonial abuses. The Spanish Gentlemen are elegantly dressed in woven shawls, wide-brimmed hats, lace-edged shirts, and velvet breeches trimmed in gold braid. The Spanish Ladies (men dressed as women) wear feathered wedding *huipiles*; they carry small bowls of Chiapanec lacquerware and a mirror, which they proudly show to all the women, bragging about how rich their husbands are. The other actors and civil officials joke with the Spanish Ladies and pretend to try to seduce them, but the Spanish Ladies will not leave their husbands. Even if he is an impotent old man, they say, he is at least wealthy enough to buy mirrors and jewelry and everything they ask for.

The Church of the Holy Martyr has never collapsed. It's never come apart. Saint Sebastian is happy there. It has a roof. It has everything.

If you ask him for grace, for blessing, if you go to him and weep, Our Lord always gives you your food. Our Lord has miracles. Our Lord is good-hearted.

On the feast day of Saint Sebastian thousands of people come to the church to make offerings and pray before the altar blanketed with masses of flowers. Next to the church is a market selling tamales, steamed chayotes, popcorn, and sweet sugarcane beer. Spooks and Jaguars walk among the crowds making rude gestures with their squirrels and proclaiming aloud the names of those members of the community who are guilty of laziness, who have refused a religious office, or who are rumored to have committed adultery. Pointing with his squirrel a Spook says, "Look also at Marian Peres from Masan! He does nothing but fornicate at the foot of the mango tree."

The Spooks run through the crowd, grabbing young boys, threatening to castrate them and boil them up for soup. The Jaguars join them in the chase, pretending they will eat the terrified boys.

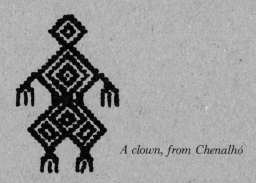

A clown, from Chenalhó

Across the field the Whiteheads, Ravens, Mossmen, and Lacandons dance together, shaking their feathered rattles, while the Spanish Gentlemen and Ladies exchange jokes with the musicians. Along the church wall scores of religious officials dressed in black wool robes sit in a row to watch the horsemen mount for the tournament. Javelins in hand, the riders charge a painted wooden stick hung between two posts. The stick is the heart of Saint Sebastian, which was never pierced by arrows; only the Zinacantecs can touch his heart.

The festival of San Sebastian celebrates the ultimate victory of the Zinacantecs over the Spanish conquistadores, for the ancient Maya traditions that were mercilessly repressed live on. Saint Sebastian has become a Zinacantec; he welcomes the ancestral gods who have come to honor him. It is also a cele-

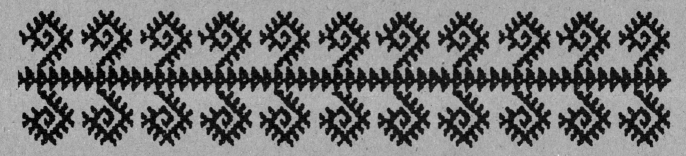

Flowery Flag, a motif from Tenejapa

bration of battles won against the Lacandons, the spooks, and jaguars. Their defeat long ago has made the world safe for humankind.

The festival of San Sebastian is also celebrated in Chiapa de Corzo by descendants of the Chiapanecs, the ancient rivals of the Zinacantecs, with whom they fought for centuries before the Spanish arrived. As part of the festival a mock battle is staged on the Grijalva River. When the English friar Thomas Gage witnessed this spectacle in 1619, he described it as a mass attack by canoes against a wooden castle. Today the battle is reenacted with a fireworks display. Boats loaded with skyrockets float down the river, shooting at an embankment that explodes into fire. The men of the town dress up as Spaniards in masks and blond wigs made out from henequen fiber. The festival commemorates the river battles fought against Zinacantecs and the conquistadores.

The Spanish Conquest and the morals of the Spaniards are both satirized in Ocozocoautla during the dance of the Moors. Brought to the New World by the Spaniards, the dance originally celebrated the final defeat of the Moors in Spain in the late fifteenth century. Saint James, the knight who led the Spaniards in early victories, is the hero of the dance. In Ocozocoautla a man wearing a horse outfit around his body (the carved horse's head before him and the tail aft) gallops about, waving a tin sword at a Moor called Mamon (Mohammed). In dance after dance Mamon is defeated by the Spanish knight. As the dance of Spanish prowess continues, dozens of men wearing blue-eyed masks with beauty marks claim in squeaky voices to be Spanish lords. These effeminate dandies parade through the streets showing off their finery—scraps of bright cloth and aluminum foil made into clothes, and stuffed animals and tin cans hanging off their belts—and throwing water balloons at one another and at the spectators. Soon the Spanish victory over the Moors breaks into a giant water fight, as the townspeople throw buckets of water from the rooftops onto the crowds below.

Some festivals mock the foreigners who have claimed power; others legitimize the power of Maya leaders. The festival of the patron saint of San Andrés, Saint Andrew, is the responsibility of the *Alférez*, or flag bearer, who serves as Saint Andrew's representative on earth. A ceremonial blessing of the flags takes place on a small platform elevated on four poles and decorated with arches of geraniums and myrtle leaves. The *Alférez*, who has purified himself through fasting and sexual abstinence, stands under the platform, removes his shirt, and strikes his back four times with a small whip, drawing a few drops of blood. He then climbs a ladder to the platform and prays over the flags, asking for divine assistance on this day.

Divine Maya kings performed a similar rite when they took office, although in those times a captive was sacrificed on the platform and the king ascended bloody steps to the throne. A bas-relief at the Maya site of Piedras Negras, Guatemala, shows the king sitting on the platform, the captive lying broken below him, and his ancestors floating above him, legitimizing his succession to the throne. Christianity has abbreviated Maya ceremonies: actual sacrifice is no longer necessary; a few drops of blood suffice.

In front of the church, straw bulls carried above the head of a dancing man announce the procession of the saints. Fireworks attached to the bull's frame spiral and explode as he dances around the plaza. The *Alférez* dances before the door of the church with the flag that is his staff of office. The statue of Saint

Andrew, arrayed in a red velvet robe and peacock feathers, is placed on a palanquin and carried from the church. Horsemen race to clear a path through the marketplace. Two groups of dancers dressed in red clash swords before the saint as he is led by the *Alférez* around the plaza.

Once a year Saint Andrew travels to the neighboring community of Magdalenas to visit his sister, Mary Magdalene. The statue is carefully packed in a wooden box and carried with a tumpline across the mountains. The ceremonial party pauses at the crosses that guard each pass, shoot fireworks, and play music to announce the coming of the saint. From the opposite direction another party brings the third member of the family, Saint Martha, the patron saint of the community of Santa Marta. When the parties reach town, they remove the saints from their boxes, put them onto palanquins, parade them around the central square, and finally set them to rest in the church. The exchange of saints, which occurs throughout Chiapas, formalizes the social and economic bonds among isolated communities. Since their saints are related, the people must be as well.

Esquipulas on the cross, from San Andrés

The following week Saint Martha and Saint Magdalene come to San Andrés to celebrate the festival of Esquipulas. The name of the festival comes from the Greek god of medicine, Aesclepius, who cured his patients through dreams; his staff with entwining snakes, the caduceus, is the modern symbol of physicians. Why Esquipulas is also the name of the Maya vision of a black Christ descending on a flaming cross is a mystery, but paintings beside the altar in Magdalenas attest to Esquipulas's miraculously healing power. Since Esquipulas is also Christ on the Cross, his festival is part of the Lenten celebrations that precede Holy Week.

The solemn reenactment of the passion of Christ during Holy Week strictly follows Spanish Catholic teachings. Although the Maya have refused to discard ancient beliefs, their faith in Christ is unwavering, and the Maya have added little from their ancient traditions to the observance of Holy Week.

On Holy Thursday in San Andrés, the statue of Christ is put in jail, a cage made of woven cane inside the church, and guarded by "soldiers" carrying muskets. On Good Friday the statue is bathed in flower water while elders raise a huge wooden cross in the center of the church. Pine trees strung with bromeliads fill the apse. Along the sides of the church sit rows of men and boys wearing crowns of chamomile flowers; they represent the Holy Ancestors, there to witness the crucifixion. The statues of the saints have been draped with purple cloth so that they will not see and be frightened by Christ's ordeal. At one o'clock, the statue of Christ is lifted up to the cross. Silver nails are inserted into the hands and feet as the people of San Andrés pray and weep for the dead Christ. At three in the afternoon the statue is taken down and laid in a casket.

Two-faced Judas design, from Pantelhó

On Saturday an effigy of Judas, which has been hanging on the church belfry, is brought down and burned. Judas wears the clothes of a Ladino, his body stuffed and bulging—a lewd, ridiculous figure. On Easter Sunday the Holy Ancestors and the religious officials sit down at a long table for a ritual meal to celebrate the resurrection of Christ.

In Chiapas the dead return each year to visit the earth not on Halloween but two days later, on the festival of *Yolon Santo*, the "Saints Below," or, as it is known throughout Mexico, the Day of the Dead. To the Maya the dead are neither frightening nor far away; they live in the earth below. Until recently the Maya buried their dead under their houses. The souls of the dead who sinned in life may have to pass time in *Katibak*, the "Burning Bones," a kind of purgatory that eventually leads to heaven where they live much as they did on earth, but without suffering.

On the second of November, All Souls' Day, families go to the graveyards with food, flowers, and incense to spend the day with their dead relatives. In Chamula, musicians wander through the graveyard playing guitar while families cover the graves with marigolds. A woman prays that the dead will come home and eat the meal that she has prepared for them:

Have their souls departed toward us?
  Have their spirits commenced to return?
Those of our forebears,
  Those of our ancestors?
Oh, Father!
  Oh, Mother!
Find your way to our house,
  Find your way to the humble place of our
    wealth.
Come and eat a bit of cabbage,
  Come and take a bit of turnip green.
Come and savor the essence of your candles,
  Come and savor the essence of your flowers.
My Lord,
  Jesus,
Release and send us the soul of our father,
  Release and send us the soul of our mother.
Rise up, Savior,
  Rise up Emmanuel.
Come and see our house,

Come and see the humble place of our wealth,
Father,
  Mother.

The belief that the dead are close by is a comfort to the survivors, who revere and respect their dead relatives. Sometimes the dead will speak and give advice. Manuel Arias of Chenalhó tells this story about visiting the graveyard on the Day of the Dead.

My grand-uncle spoke to José Arias Sohom, his son, through a little saint in a gourd. It was his father's own voice that was heard and he called him Yuxep (José):
"How are you, my children?"
"Come in, your food is here" (answered Yuxep).
"You know, Yuxep, you know that you are still young, easily roused to anger and a little jealous. That is not good. I, who used to beat your mother and sinned greatly, have had my arms and penis taken off. We are in great danger of Katibak.*"*

During Carnaval men dressed as the dead come to chastise the living. Carnaval is celebrated in Catholic countries with wild feasts that precede Lent. At the time of the Spanish Conquest the five lost days of the Maya calendar roughly coincided with Carnaval. In Chamula the Maya calendar is adjusted yearly to ensure that Carnaval will occur during *Ch'ay K'in*— the five lost days—regarded as a time when bad luck and evil spirits walk upon the earth and the world is turned upside down. The festival begins with the sacrifice of an animal and ends with a sign of new life.

In Chenalhó, Carnaval begins at noon on Sunday, when two turkeys are strung up on a rope above the street. They are hung like the stick that represents the heart of Saint Sebastian. Turkeys, however, are not saints. Men on horseback gallop by, pulling out handfuls of feathers from the live birds. After three passes, the turkeys are taken down, and their heads are chopped off by men painted in black, who call themselves the Dead.

The Dead sling the plucked turkeys over their backs and, followed by a group of musicians, proceed to the house of a religious official. They stand outside the house and shout, "Woop, woop, woop, we are the Dead." All the people in the house pretend to be afraid and go hide in the corners. I watched the Dead walk in, demand a table and chairs, sit down, and fling the two turkeys' bodies on the table.

"Oh, I think that this is my father," one said. "Oh, my brothers, oh, fellow dead, it's my uncle. He's dead; oh, he's gone. We must pray over the dead." Saying, "Mumbly, gumbly, oogly, boogly," the Dead made the sign of the cross backwards and sideways.

"My uncle, wouldn't you like a little bit to drink?" asked one. They poured some *posh* into the beak of one of the turkeys.

Another asked, "My uncle, wouldn't you like a cigarette?" He put a lit cigarette into the other turkey's beak.

The two turkey heads started to fight. The Dead said, "That's just as it's always been in life!"

By their actions the Dead shame those who do not know how to pray, who instead of offering their ancestors food at the graveyard go only to smoke and drink. The chance that they too may be reprimanded by the Dead, and perhaps stand alone on this earth without the guidance of the Ancestors, horrifies the spectators.

That night the transvestites appear. All the men in the community have borrowed skirts and *huipiles* from their wives or mothers and wander as a group from house to house, dancing and singing, "I am half a woman, I am half a girl." In a somewhat remarkable, unselfconscious exhibition of their feminine side, the men seem happy to play the female chorus. The evening is surprisingly free of ribald humor.

Monday is the opposite, for the wild Lacandons are the focus of the celebration. Those impersonating Lacandon men have white circles and crosses painted on their bodies. With their Lacandon women—men dressed in striped shawls and ceremonial *huipiles*—they wander through the crowds pretending to cure people by stroking them with leafy branches.

Events are relatively tame until dusk, when four Lacandon women rush into the house of a religious official and ask for refuge. They lie down in the middle of the floor, and a mat is thrown over them. A few minutes later four men playing a Ladino hunter and his dogs race in, searching for the women. They poke into every corner, check the rafters, and peer into the faces of the women in the house, asking, "Are you the women, are you the ones we are looking for?" Finally, one of the "dogs" discovers the mat in the middle of the floor, raises up one corner and shouts, "I found them!" The mat is flung off and the hunter and his dogs proceed to jump on the women, imitating copulation. The Lacandon women protest, saying, "It shouldn't be like that," and they throw the men down and do the same to them. Then all rise and address the children, who have been watching this scene intently, telling them, "This is how it is done, watch carefully, this is how it is done."

It is said that at the beginning of the world people did not know how to have sex, and God was too embarrassed to show them. So the devil told the first man to watch him and learn while he made love to his wife. The skit of the Lacandon women keeps the devil out of the fun.

Performing inside the religious officials' houses would be impossible in Chamula, where thousands of people come to watch the festivities. Carnaval in Chamula is called *K'in Tahimoltik*, "the Festival of Games," but the games there are not the morality plays of Chenalhó.

First sacrificial bulls are brought to the homes of the three *Pasiónes*, the leaders of the festival, and slaughtered. In front of each *Pasión*'s house is hung a bull's head, with the skin of the lower jaw removed, a sign of the death of the beast. A fleshless lower jaw was the ancient Maya hieroglyph for death. The bull's body is left lying in the courtyard. Each *Pasión* and his assistants line up to bite the flesh above the heart. All taste the death of a powerful enemy; bulls wreaked havoc centuries ago when Spanish ranchers let their animals graze through Maya cornfields. When bulls appear later in the Carnaval they will be tamed.

A long-limbed Max, *from San Andrés*

Monkeys, the people of the previous creation, come elegantly dressed to lead the games. *Maxetik*, as the Monkeys are called, wear a version of a seventeenth-century military costume first worn by French grenadiers, which includes a frock coat and leather breeches. The beaverskin hat has been exchanged for one of howler monkey fur festooned with long ribbons. Any man who can afford to dress up for the occasion can become a *Max*. Monkeys dance through the crowds, playing guitar and accordian, singing, and making rude jokes with the cooks and religious officials. The *Maxetik's* songs are improvised as they are sung continually throughout the festival; one *Max* sings of the saints, covered with Lenten shrouds:

Cover the eyes,
  Cover the face
Of Our Lord in Heaven,
  Of Our Lord in Glory.
Oh, you know of his goodness,
  Oh you know of his greatness,

Of the Lord of Heaven,
  Of the Lord of Glory.
Your festival has come;
  Your goodness has come, Lord of Heaven.
For only three days of your greatness,
  For only three days of your goodness,
For only three days of your festival,
  Lord of Heaven.
horoho — horoho — horoho.

The *Maxetik* are major participants in the reenactment of a legendary war between Chiapas and Guatemala. In a number of myths Guatemala is a land of demons who eat people. During the colonial period, when Chiapas was part of Guatemala, Maya who were sent to the capital during the Inquisition rarely returned. In the mock battle monkeys and men divide into two armies, name their captains and sergeants, and gather up the horse manure as they stand on opposing hills. With a shout they rush each other, throwing dung. In the final onslaught, Guatemala and the demons are defeated.

The major spectacle is held the next day, Shrove Tuesday. In preparation, the Flowery Monkeys, who are the *Pasión's* personal assistants, lead a gang of young boys off to collect bundles of thatch, while the ritual assistants sweep a wide path from the church to the cross at the western end of the plaza. When the thatch has been gathered, the religious officials, Monkeys, flag bearers, and dozens of boys race around the plaza three times, waving banners and blowing trumpets, pausing to pray at the crosses at each of the four corners. Finally, the *Pasiónes* wait at the cross in front of the church while the boys lay thatch along the swept path across the plaza under the watchful eyes of the Flowery Monkeys. If any dog makes the mistake of walking on this path it is beaten back by the Monkeys, who carry whips made of bull penises. The crowd stands alongside the path waiting. At noon the thatch is lit, and the *Pasiónes* lead their successors and the Flowery Monkeys through the smoke and flames three times in an act of purification that will draw the sun along this same burning path until next year's celebration.

After the firewalk, bulls are led into the plaza on long ropes, each held by twenty men. The bulls are pulled through the shouting crowd that swirls around them. Occasionally, a man will try to mount and ride one. After they have been paraded about to show that the beasts are now harmless, they are returned to pasture.

On Ash Wednesday, after the crowds have returned home, the *Pasiónes* meet on the steps of the church to begin the cycle of Lenten celebrations and to officially conclude Carnaval. The demons have been defeated, the religious officials have atoned for the sins of the community, and the sun is set in motion for the new year.

Maya festivals celebrate each year's victory over the forces that threaten their world. On the saint's day the old gods and demons reappear to admonish those who have forgotten the true and proper way of behaving. The ancient traditions that are subtly preserved in myths, weaving, and daily life come alive in the theater and ritual of the festivals. The Ancestors in dreams and the flowery face of God at noon watch over their people who live at the center of the world.

Celebrating the Demons' Defeat

In praise of "the flowery face of Our Father"—the sun—and the saints in heaven, a religious official from Tenejapa offers a flowering bromeliad, an air plant that lives for months separated from the branches of a living tree. The Maya celebrate each holy day with the rituals of their ancestors. They are Christian—they believe in the power of Christ and the saints and follow the religious practices taught by Spanish missionaries 450 years ago—but their saints are Maya: they appear in visions and dreams to confirm the special grace of their people. Closely related to the saints are the Holy Ancestors, their confidants and companions, who live in the mountains above each community and protect their people from the demons and witches who would steal their souls. The Ancestors call men and women to sit at their table, where they learn how to set bones, cure the sick, and play the music for the festivals of the saints.

ABOVE: When Cortéz placed the first cross in the New World in the early sixteenth century, he instructed the Maya to honor it with prayers and flowers. The Chamula family lighting a candle before their house cross keeps alive the faith, which has gained a Maya interpretation. Christ, the light of the world, is seen daily in the form of the sun. A cross is placed on the eastern wall of every Maya home to commemorate the risen Christ and the rising sun; on the patio another cross faces west to salute the sun's passage below the earth.

OPPOSITE: Mol Domingo, a shaman from Chamula, once led the festival of Santa Rosario in his community, and still keeps a statue of the saint in his home. Just as in the church, the statue is draped with layers of flowery cloth to keep it warm, and it wears a ribbon necklace with a mirror as a jewel. Mol Domingo's reflection in the saint's mirror is a casual sign of his personal devotion to Santa Rosario.

Shamans pray to the saints to intercede with God and to the Ancestors, who guard each person's animal companion spirit in their mountain caves. If a person ignores his duty to the community by lack of devotion to the saints or personal sin, the Ancestors will cease to care for his animal spirit and he will become ill, causing him to send for a shaman. Mol Domingo, like all other shamans, was summoned in his dreams to the council of Ancestors, who taught him what offerings should be made and which words used to plead for his patient's restoration to health.

OVERLEAF: In his second home, in Chamula center, Mol Domingo receives patients and discusses with them the causes of their illness. If it is a physical disease he will refer the patient to a medical doctor, but if after listening to a patient's pulse he determines that a part of his or her soul has been lost, he will pray to the saints and Ancestors on his patient's behalf.

A Zinacantec curing ceremony involves the patient's immediate family and other close relatives, who, as ritual assistants, prepare food, gather flowers and candles for the cross shrines, and collect water from seven holy springs to bathe the patient before he is presented to the Ancestors.

ABOVE: Before going to the seven mountaintop shrines to pray for the return of his patient's soul, Anselmo Perez, a Zinacantec shaman, shares a ritual meal of chicken soup with his assistants.

OPPOSITE: Burning copal incense, Anselmo prays for his patient's recovery in front of the flowers he will bring to the mountaintop shrines:

> *Thy child, thy offspring,*
> *Thy bloom, thy sprout,*
> *Take heed, My Father, Take heed, My Lord!*
> *For this I prod thy Lordly nostrils, For this I prod thy Lordly ears,*
> *What now shall be decided? What now shall be weighed?*

The patient lies behind Anselmo on a mattress of pine needles and a pillow of sweet herbs and flowers.

OVERLEAF: At the crosses of the shrine at Calvario, where the Ancestors meet to decide the fate of their people, Anselmo prays with his ritual assistants and patient, asking, "Will he still enjoy, will he still delight, in thy beauteous Lordly faces, in thy beauteous Lordly eyes?"

ABOVE: Kneeling on a carpet of pine, Zinacantec families pray in the chapel of the hamlet of Choktoj. With festival banners hung on its rafters and icons of the saints placed among flowers on the altar, the chapel evokes the image of heaven on earth.

OPPOSITE: The ruined wall of a colonial church masks still another church in Carranza. Beyond the steeple, a chapel stands next to a cieba tree that shaded the marketplace of Carranza long before the arrival of the church: the True Cross stands next to the Maya symbol of the Tree of Life.

ABOVE: Bishops and other clergy, seen here satirized by masqueraders in Suchiapa, were at times more interested in personal gain than in the salvation of souls. Although the first bishop of Chiapas was renowned for his compassion, and the present bishop has dedicated himself to helping the poor, others, especially during the colonial period, became wealthy by demanding alms and high fees for baptisms and marriages. Such actions nullified the authority of the church hierarchy in the eyes of the Maya, who now choose their own leaders.

OPPOSITE: The *Pasiónes* of Chenalhó, husband and wife, will lead their community through the raucous festival of Carnaval before Lent and the solemn celebration of the passion of Christ during Holy Week. Each saint in the church is served for one year by a designated couple, who are responsible for biweekly offerings of flowers and incense as well as for preparing the candles, food, and drink for the festival in the saint's honor.

ABOVE: *Capitánes* of Tenejapa carry the red banners and shaved sticks of their office as they dance in time with the flutist in a circuit around town during Carnaval. Five days and nights of prayer and ceremony become a physical and spiritual test of each *Capitán*, who must lead the festival like a captain in battle.

OPPOSITE: The flag bearers, or *Alféreces*, of Amatenango emerge from the church in pairs representing the two districts of the community. The first pair, having concluded a year of service to a saint, are about to pass on to the second pair the bundles containing the saint's possessions.

ABOVE: The wisdom of the elders is both mocked and confirmed during a Christmas theatre led by Grandfathers, wearing long, red masks, and Grandmothers, in white veils. The painted mat "bull" is the Grandparents' prized animal and the main prop in a burlesque comdedy that reveals the consequences of foolish behavior.

OPPOSITE: A *Max*, or monkey, of Chamula is dressed in a ribboned howler monkey-fur hat and a red-trimmed military frock coat. For the three days of Carnaval the *Maxetik* sing, dance, make rude jokes, and act like the people of the first creation, who refused to obey God and were turned into monkeys for their improper behavior.

ABOVE: Wearing their finest tinsel and smooth pale masks, the boys of Ocozocoautla claim to be Spanish Lords during Carnaval. Mocking the virility and morals of the conquistadores, and speaking in high falsetto voices, one offers a recital on a toy violin and another introduces a dead monkey as his child.

OPPOSITE: During Carnaval the world is turned upside down. The men of Chenalhó don women's clothing and sing in chorus at each religious official's house, "I am half a woman, I am half a girl." They neither imitate nor mock women, but simply acknowledge the feminine side of all men.

ABOVE: Zinacantec clowns lead a brass band playing German polkas into the plaza at Pasté. Such bands were a mark of high culture in Mexico a century ago. Zinacantecs keep up the tradition while they mock those aspects of Mexican culture they abhor: one clown is a "politician" in red pants and the wide hat of a revolutionary soldier; another is a "Ladina woman" clutching her illegitimate child while high stepping in a mini-skirt.

OPPOSITE: Skyrockets are shot off to announce important occasions and each movement of a festival so that the whole town will know when the clowns are arriving or the procession of the saints is about to begin. The cane cylinders, packed with gunpowder and a bomb at one head, normally shoot straight up but occasionally fly horizontally, scattering the crowds in their path. Standing on a far hill this man from Tenejapa sends up an announcement of the arrival of the governor of Chiapas to a political meeting.

ABOVE: A Zinacantec spectator glances away as the "bull" and the clowns approach the kiosk of Pasté. The man inside the bull is shielded from the flares and bombs tied to the frame which send cascades of sparks and smoke into the crowds.

OPPOSITE: The saints emerge from the church at Chamula, their gold crowns and haloes shining in the sunlight above a cloud of gunpowder. Accompanied by religious officials bearing their flags of office, the saints are carried around the atrium of the church to witness their people celebrating. After the procession men line up to embrace the statue of Santa Rosario and dance with her in the church.

ABOVE: Musicians and *Capitánes* herd a mat "bull" in the streets of Tenejapa during Carnaval, symbolically taming the beast that used to devastate their cornfields centuries ago when Spanish colonists routinely grazed their cattle on Maya land.

OPPOSITE: In the Maya calendar, Carnaval marks the end of the year; live turkeys are sacrificed to pay for the sins of the past and to bring in the new year. In Chenalhó (above) religious officials race under the sacrificial turkeys, pulling out handfuls of feathers on each pass. In San Andrés (below) the Black Monkey, a demonic figure of Carnaval, chews the head he bit off the turkey while it was hanging above the street.

OVERLEAF: In Tenejapa the animals of sacrifice are represented by mock bulls, which become children's playthings at the end of the festival. Real bulls are actually sacrificed in Chamula, but at the end of Carnaval live bulls are paraded through town as symbolic replacements and set out to pasture as a sign of the new year.

PRECEDING PAGES: Dawn over the Chamula graveyard at Romerio. On the Day of the Dead families bring food and drink to the cemetery to share a meal with their deceased relatives.

ABOVE: Musicians, called to service through dreams, play the steady rhythm of the festivals and help guide the religious officials through their year of ritual duties.

OPPOSITE: The bundle embraced by a *Martoma* in Tenejapa holds past offerings of clothing and necklaces that are now too worn to be placed on the saint. The bundle is the symbol of the burden of religious office—to preserve the devotion of past generations and pass it on to next year's guardians.

BELOW: In his home made holy with music and flowers, a Tenejapan *Martoma* calls upon God to accept his humble offerings.

Epilogue

Maya culture will soon disappear. Who can resist the tide of progress? Ever since the nineteenth century foreigners have confidently predicted that Maya culture and religion would soon become "civilized" and European; now that television has arrived in Chiapas, observers are certain that the Maya will leave behind the traditions that make them a distinct people in the rush to become like the rest of the Western world.

My Maya friends were shocked when I mentioned the idea to them.

"It can't be, because there is a difference, a difference given to each of us by Our Lord," said Rosha Hernandez of San Andrés.

"I feel that I am more Maya than ever, because it is all that I have," said Pedro Meza, a Tenejapan Maya, while waiting in the San Antonio airport for his flight back to Mexico. Pedro had just finished mounting his third exhibition of Chiapas textiles in the United States. "I have no desire to belong to another culture," he continued. "I think that it is very good to talk with you and with others as friends—strange people, interesting people, people from other places, other traditions, many traditions. But it is impossible to be like these people of other traditions. There are times when my people don't understand this. They want to get something pretty—a tape recorder or something like that—but those are things, and it is impossible to be like a thing."

Pedro Meza is the director of Sna Jolobil, the Maya weavers' society of Chiapas. Rosha is the master weaver of her community. The weavers' society is one of the ways in which the Maya are preserving their traditions in the twentieth century. Another is a writers' workshop known as Sna jTz'ibajom, where Anselmo Perez and other men publish books in Tzotzil and Tzeltal Maya. Maya society uses modern means to preserve its language and culture while the people continue to heed the dreams of the saints and Ancestors. The Maya have over 450 years of practice in how to survive hard times.

OPPOSITE: The wife of the *Alférez* of Amatenango remains as silent as the statue of the Holy Virgin during Carnaval. Although women do not lead the public ceremonies, their role is considered to be as vital as that of their husbands, for it is they who oversee the crew of ritual assistants and cooks who make the festival possible.

The people of Chiapas still face some critical problems. Most of the lands stolen from them during the nineteenth century were never returned, despite the promises of the Mexican Revolution. Hydroelectric dams built in the last two decades to provide power to Mexico City have flooded entire lowland villages out of existence and made farmland even more scarce. Ninety percent of the good farmland is owned by ten percent of the people, in a state where the per capita income averages three hundred dollars a year. Reclaiming lost land is a bitter struggle: dozens of lives are lost each year in violent land disputes.

Scarcity of land is compounded by a recent population explosion, which has forced families to leave their homes in the Highlands and form colonies in the Lacandon jungle. They follow the logging roads to a patch of forest where the biggest trees have been leveled and burn the remaining vegetation for cornfields. After a few years the soil becomes depleted of nutrients, and the land is sold off to cattle ranchers for grassland, leaving the people homeless once again. The same destructive cycle occurs in the Grijalva Valley, where the Maya traditionally rented small plots for their cornfields. Landowners have found it more profitable to raise cattle for export than to lease their land to farmers. Soon there will be few areas in the lowland and jungle to which the Maya can migrate and grow their corn. Land disputes will become far more prevalent—and more serious—before they are resolved.

Social and economic pressures in the community have erupted in political conflicts. The limited resources are not evenly distributed, and government aid, in the form of trucks, road- and school-building contracts, terracing projects, and the like, is often monopolized by a few powerful families for private gain. These families nominate the political officials of the town and promote traditional festivals to justify their preeminence in the community.

The disenfranchised sometimes join opposing political parties or convert to evangelical sects to avoid paying local taxes and supporting the festivals, which require great sacrifices of time and money. The evangelical missionaries, as the Spanish missionaries did centuries before them, impose their own culture along with their religion. Embracing Western materialsm, evangelical Maya hope to drive to heaven in a new car. In response the traditional leaders of Chamula expelled all evangelists from the community. Other communities remain divided, with traditional and evangelical factions vying for power.

In the midst of these upheavals some things in Chiapas are improving. The rate of alcoholism in Maya communities has dropped drastically in the last decade. Ten years ago the roads leading out from the centers of towns after a market day or festival would be littered with drunks, their wives waiting patiently beside them until they were sober enough to walk home. The excessive drinking once required of festival participants is now frowned upon: soda pop has become an acceptable substitute for *posh* in the ceremonies, and those who choose to drink alcohol generally drink moderately. It is now common to see Maya shamans offering Coca-Cola instead of *posh* at curing ceremonies conducted in church.

Drunken toad, from San Andrés

Ambitious development programs by the Mexican government have also affected the Highlands in the last decade. The primary schools and health clinics built in each community and many of the outlying hamlets are too understaffed to be truly effective, but a new network of paved roads has improved the economic situation there. Farmers can now truck their vegetables and flowers directly to market, sometimes bypassing the local markets entirely to sell their produce at higher prices in Mexico City. More important, the roads have relieved the threat of famine, as corn is brought to government distribution centers throughout the Highlands. The roads have brought a measure of wealth and security to communities that are no longer self-sufficient in basic goods. Most families have at least one wage earner now, and money has replaced the barter of farm goods in the market.

"In the past, we wove everything," explained Rosha. "Even the children's diapers were made of cotton that we spun and wove. We didn't buy anything; we did not have a bit of money. When we ran out of beans we ate our tortillas with a little salt, and maybe chile, that was all. Now people buy their vegetables and maybe a little meat in the market. Everyone buys their corn now; you see them carrying kilos of corn home from the market. We eat bought food."

The change from a sustenance to a monetary economy is clearly manifested in dramatic changes in costume. Chamula women once all wore black wool shawls, but in the mid-1970s less expensive, brightly colored acrylic shawls became popular. For a few years women wore shawls of every hue, until the community came to a consensus that blue was the proper color. The choice was not arbitrary but based on a traditional antecedent—the blue ceremonial *huipiles* preserved since the nineteenth century. On market day in Chamula the plaza is a sea of blue shawls. What was at first a foreign influence became integrated into the costume and identity of the community.

When I began my research on Maya textiles, *huipiles* brocaded with complex designs were common, but brocading gradually became rare as women took up embroidery. I became very concerned about the apparent loss of traditional weaving. When a woman showed me a blouse she had made with an embroidered kangaroo, I decided to organize Sna Jolobil, the weavers' society, to save a dying art. My

efforts were helpful, but the sense of tradition in Maya culture proved stronger. After a few years of experimentation kangaroos and other strange mutations of textile design disappeared, and the women looked to traditional models, just as the three women from Tenejapa had done at the turn of the century. The ancient brocade designs are now copied even in embroidery. Maya *huipiles* today are brighter and the designs more innovative, but they are recognizably of the same tradition as those worn by their ancient ancestors.

Weavers have always had the saints' *huipiles* as models to study, but historically in times of great change they have formed societies to help preserve weaving, as when after the turn of the century a dozen women in Tenejapa formed a religious society that wove *huipiles* for the saints and religious officials. Thus more *huipiles* were available for study, and brocading was quickly learned by the whole community. Sna Jolobil performs a similar function. It maintains a study collection of traditional weavings, gives stipends to weavers who wish to study and recreate the old motifs, and promotes the sale of its members' work. Its workshop on natural dyes has been experimenting with local plants for years and recreates the dyeing techniques that were lost for a generation. Silk brocade *huipiles* that were last woven a century ago have been studied and the patterns and techniques revived. The weavers' society has encouraged a renaissance of the ancient art.

I think that had I not helped to create Sna Jolobil the Maya probably would have organized something similar by themselves. Sna Jolobil is now run solely by Maya weavers. One of the more succesful Maya cultural institutions, it was strongly supported by the Mexican government. Mexico's President Miguel de la Madrid presented Sna Jolobil with the National Award for Arts and Sciences in December 1986 in recognition of its work in preserving Maya weaving traditions.

Without the assistance and patience of the women

of Sna Jolobil it would have been impossible to take the photographs in this book.

The Maya regard photographers as subtle thieves. Photographers "steal their souls"—an apt metaphor for that moment when a total stranger snaps one's picture and walks on without saying a word. The act of taking a picture can be not only abusive, but also exploitative. People in the Highlands reason that photographers must be making a lot of money from those pictures; how else could they afford to be carrying around equipment that would cost a Maya two years' wages? When a photographer tries to be a neutral observer, detached and invisible behind his camera, the Maya tend to throw stones to get his attention.

The Maya of Chiapas have never been fond of photographers. Their distrust of the camera started long before tourism brought busloads of French and German vacationers to see the festivals. The first anthropologist to travel to Chiapas, Fredrick Starr, used especially disagreeable methods to secure documentation for his research in 1902. Starr wanted to measure and photograph the heads of the women of Chamula but found them most unwilling. No matter how persistent he was, the Maya women refused to enter his studio. Exasperated, Starr had his assistant run through the market and grab women's shawls. The women, protesting loudly, chased him into the studio, where Starr waited with his camera.

When Jeffrey Foxx began to take photographs of the Maya in 1977, he did not receive a warm reception. As he relates:

I asked, begged, groveled in turkey shit, used guile, gave presents, beseeched, hid, climbed, and drove great distances to get good pictures. I tried hard. In the face of severe disappointments I expected there would be a positive turn of events. In a universal sense I believed I was at one with the people, and yet I was in awe of the differences that could never be overcome. I was taken by the beauty of the people and their dignity. I had respect for the simple and complex solutions of their culture to perpetuate itself.

It has become progressively more difficult to shoot in the Highlands. Every hotel in San Cristóbal now has signs posted prohibiting photography in Chamula and Zinacantan. In one sense this is a positive sign: the people refuse to be intimidated by foreigners. Some Maya understand a need for documentation in the face of rapid change, but others see the camera as the symbol of the intrusion of the outside world and seek to ban it from the community that they wish to preserve. The pressure is so intense that Maya fear being seen cooperating with a photographer in public, yet I was often invited to photograph families in their homes.

Obviously the person behind the camera counts for something. Over the years Jeffrey earned the trust of the Maya, particularly the women of Sna Jolobil, who brought him into their communities. The people Jeffrey photographed proudly display their family portraits next to the house altar.

As documents, photographs have occasionally proven useful to the community. After the Church of San Lorenzo was destroyed by fire, the religious officials of Zinacantan searched for old photographs of the altar to make sure that it would be rebuilt exactly as it had been. In the same way, the textile collections of Sna Jolobil have been useful in preserving designs that may have been forgotten in time. Documentation is important, but I suspect that the Maya would have rebuilt the church correctly and revived brocade without collections of photographs and weavings.

The Chamulas, for instance, are now building pyramids. They did not go to the ruins and decide to copy them; they simply arrived at a moment when they have enough people and money to create monumental architecture once again. Since these structures are being built to honor their ancestors and community, just as the earlier pyramids were, it is not surprising that they are similar in form as well as meaning. The Chamulas are making the pyramids by terraforming the three sacred mountains, all called Calvario, around Chamula center. Each of

Ancient house, from Zinacantan

these mountains has on its top a cross shrine to the Ancestors of the three districts of Chamula. Platforms have been built on the summit around the shrine, and wide sets of stairs rise from the base of the hills, giving the appearance of pyramids with crosses on top.

The Maya have lived in the same area for thousands of years with the same beliefs as their ancestors. In a sense their own cyclical view of time has been confirmed by the revival of ancient architecture. This does not mean that Chamula is about to reenter the Classic period. The world has changed, but the Maya view of what is proper and sacred has remained the same.

Traveling to the center of Chamula today one still passes by thatch-roofed houses and cornfields; the trip, however, is no longer a two-hour hike but more likely a fifteen-minute drive in a microbus crammed with Chamulas and driven, as fast as possible, by a young man who keeps the tape deck blaring at full volume. But the music, surprisingly, is ritual harp, guitar, and violin melodies that the driver recorded himself at the last festival. And he or another member of his family still tends the patch of holy corn next to his house.

The strength of Maya traditions comes from living in tight-knit communities, where all decisions must be agreed upon and accepted by all its members. There are moments when the society opens up to new ideas, like the varieties of brightly colored shawls, only to retreat to a common agreement on what is proper. The most important source of inspiration is dreams; like Mol Comate's vision of the flaming cross above Chenalhó, dreams bring the individual into direct contact with the saints and Ancestors who have guided Maya communities since the beginning of the world. These dreams are shared and can be confirmed by others in the community. When a shaman dreams of meeting the Ancestors, other shamans will dream of the same meeting, and the new shaman will appear in their dreams. When the saint in Tenejapa asked for a *huipil*, three women had the same dream, and each set off to learn brocade. The whole community dreams together.

When I discussed the role of Sna Jolobil in preserving Maya tradition with Pedro Meza, he turned to me and said: "It is wrong to say that one is reaffirming a tradition, it's not like that. Really, it is the dream that has returned. There is nothing to reaffirm; it is given."

Selected Bibliography

Anawalt, Patricia Rieff. *Indian Clothing before Cortés; Mesoamerican Costumes from the Codices*. The Civilization of the American Indians Series, no. 156. Norman: University of Oklahoma Press, 1981.

Burstein, John; Past, Amber; and Waserstrom, Robert. *Slo'il Jchi'iltaktik (En sus proprias palabras, Cuarto vidas Tzotziles)*. Mexico, D.F.: C.A.D.A.L., 1979.

Bricker, Victoria. *Ritual Humor in the Highlands of Chiapas*. Austin: University of Texas Press, 1973.

Coe, Michael. *The Maya*. London: Thames and Hudson, 1984.

Cordry, Donald Bush, and Cordry, Dorothy M. *Costumes and Weaving of the Zoque Indians of Chiapas, Mexico*. Southwest Museum Papers Number Fifteen. Los Angeles: Southwest Museum, 1941.

———. *Mexican Indian Costumes*. Austin: University of Texas Press, 1968.

Díaz, Bernal. *The Conquest of New Spain*. New York: Penguin Books, 1963.

Díaz, Bernal, del Castillo. *Historia Verdadera de la conquista de la Nueva Espana*. Vol. 2. Mexico, D.F.: Editorial del Valle de Mexico, 1976.

Ekholm, Susanna. "The Lagartero Figurines." In *Maya Archaeology and Ethno-history*. Edited by Normand Hammond and Gordon Willey. Austin: University of Texas Press, 1979.

Gossen, Gary. *Chamulas in the World of the Sun*. Cambridge, Mass.: Harvard University Press, 1974.

Graham, Ian, and Von Euw, Eric. *Corpus of Maya Hieroglyphic Inscriptions*. Vol. 3, Part 1. Cambridge, Mass.: Peabody Museum of Archaeology and Ethnology, Harvard University, 1977.

Guiterez-Holmes, Calixta. *Perils of the Soul*. New York: The Free Press of Glencoe, 1961.

Laughlin, Robert. *People of the Bat*. Edited by Carol Karasik. Washington, D.C.: Smithsonian Institution Press, 1987.

———. *Of Shoes and Ships and Sealing Wax*. Smithsonian Contributions to Anthropology, No. 25. Washington, D.C.: Smithsonian Institution Press, 1980.

Lechuga, Ruth D. *El Traje indígena de México*. Mexico, D.F.: Panorama Editoral, S.A., 1982.

Morris, Walter F., Jr. "Flowers, Saints and Toads: Ancient and Modern Maya Textile Design Symbolism." *National Geographic Research*. Washington, D.C.: National Geographic Society, 1985.

———. "Maya Time Warps." *Archaeology*. New York, 1986.

———. *A Millennium of Weaving in Chiapas*. San Cristóbal de Las Casas: Sna Jolobil, 1984.

Morris, Walter F., Jr., and Meza, Pedro M. *Luchetik: The Woven Word from Highland Chiapas*. San Cristóbal de Las Casas: Sna Jolobil and Editorial "Fray Bartolomé de Las Casas," A.C., 1980.

Schele, Linda, and Miller, Mary Ellen. *The Blood of Kings: Dynasty and Ritual in Maya Art*. New York: George Braziller and Kimbell Art Museum, 1986.

Sna Jtz'ibajom. *Los Antiguos comerciantes zinacantecos (Vo'ne jchonolajetik ta Tzinakanta)*. San Cristóbal de Las Casas: Secretaría de Educación y Cultura and Subsecretaría de Cultura y Recreación, 1984.

———. *Historia antigua de Zinacantán (Vo'ne k'op ta Tzinakanta)*. San Cristóbal de Las Casas: Subsecretaria de Cultura y Recreación, 1983.

———. *El Primer soldado llego á Chamula (Ba' yel soltaro vul ta Chamula)*. San Cristóbal de Las Casas: Subsecretaría de Cultura y Recreación, 1983.

———. *Ya'yejik te mamaletik (Palabras de los ancianos)*. San Cristóbal de Las Casas: Secretaría de Educación y Cultura and Subsecretaría de Cultura y Recreación, 1983.

Starr, Frederick. *In Indian Mexico*. Chicago: Forbes & Co., 1908.

Stephens, John L. *Incidents of Travel in Central America, Chiapas, and Yucatán*. New York: Dover Publications, 1969.

Stuart, George E., and Stuart, Gene S. *The Mysterious Maya*. Washington, D.C.: National Geographic Society, 1977.

Tedlock, Dennis. *Popol Vuh*. New York: Simon & Schuster, 1985.

Thompson, J. Erik. *Thomas Gage's Travel to the New World*. Norman: University of Oklahoma Press, 1958.

Vos, Jan de. *La Paz del Dios y del Rey*. Estado de Chiapas: Colección Cieba, 1980.

Waserstrom, Robert. *Class and Society in Central Chiapas*. Berkeley, Calif.: Academic Press, 1984.

Illustration Credits

(The authors and publishers wish to thank the following individuals who have graciously consented to the reproduction of their illustrations. References are to page numbers)
All drawings are by Pedro Meza except as noted. Sari Dor, 15; Philip Foxx, 107, 167; Ian Graham, 29, 108; Kees Grootenboer, 13, 28, 115; Marla Hooks, 106, top left and right; 109, 111 right, 112, 117 bottom, 118 left, 168, 213 bottom; Mariano López Méndez, 21, 22, 23, 157, 158, 159, 161; Mica McGuirk, 117 top; Patricia Morris, 34, 71, 116; Katherine Nigh, 66; Elizabeth Ross, 11, 12, 17, 18, 20, 24, 31, 62 left, 65, 68, 69, 70, 110, 114, 118 bottom, 119 top, 154; Linda Schele, 27

As It Was in the Beginning

There exists a myth of purity about native peoples, a feeling that the works of modern society are so powerful that contact with them will taint and defile a "primitive" culture—as though if the Chamula mother and daughter seen here were to actually pluck one of the brightly colored plastic containers from the wall they would be expelled from the Garden. The Maya are not as concerned with things as we; their daily rituals are not copies of older models but living traditions confirmed in dreams. The saints and Ancestors speak to their people of the wisdom of God when He created the world. The Maya world will continue until the dreams cease.

ABOVE: The romantic vision of Zinacantecs and all Maya people remaining frozen forever like snapshots fading in an old album wrongly assumes that the Maya have neither a future nor a past. During the five millennia of Maya history the culture has changed dramatically, but many traditions, such as the adornment of the house cross with pine boughs, are preserved and renewed. The Zinacantec child who left his toy truck at the foot of the cross will grow up to maintain his own house shrine, and probably drive a truck as well, for the Zinacantecs have the largest fleet in Chiapas.

OPPOSITE: Bulldozers crawling through the Lacandon jungle haul off mahogany from the last patch of virgin rain forest in Mexico. The destruction of the forest is causing a drought in Chiapas and will in time affect the rest of the world as well.

ABOVE: The Virgin shares the altar in a modern Chamula home with a television set, but, like the saints who came before them, the cowboys on the screen are just another layer in Maya culture. Behind the altar rest four boughs of pine, representative of the four corners of the Maya world.

OPPOSITE: Weaving in the manner she learned as a young girl, a Tenejapan elder continues to make her life beautiful with the ancient designs of a world in flower.

OVERLEAF: The television repeating station sprouting microwave dishes stands above the Earthlord's cave on Moss Mountain, where Chamula shamans pray for rain each spring. The Maya are not offended by the tower but find it appropriate that the Earthlord, the owner of the world's riches, would wish to have such a gaudy decoration with its flashing red lights illuminating his home.

Acknowledgments

Writing this book, my first, was a terrifying experience. Without Carol Karasik's cheerful support and knowledgeable critique, this book would not have been completed. Marti Malovany encouraged us to publish with Abrams, and Beverly Fazio and Michael Hentges somehow managed to remain helpful and smiling throughout the entire publishing process. Jeffrey Foxx initiated this project and has been a pleasure to work with over the last decade of excursions through Chiapas.

I would also like to thank the following individuals for sharing with me their special knowledge and expertise: Jan Rus; Robert Wasserman; Evon Z. Vogt; Jan de Vos; Eugenio Mauer, S.J.; Joe Copp; and Dennis Breedlove. Mica McGuirk, Francisco Alvarez, Francis Méndez, and John and Kathy Keegan helped me organize this and earlier works. Pedro Meza, Patricia Morris, Elizabeth Ross, Mariano López Méndez (the president of Chamula), Kees Grootenboer, Philip Foxx, and Marla Hooks, my wife, generously offered their drawings to illustrate this book. My neighbor, Trudy Blom, let me use her library and telephone; Gordon Jeffries drove me around Chiapas in his '49 pickup; and my parents have, even in the worst of times, always been supportive. The unfailing interest and encouragement of the women of Sna Jolobil have sustained my efforts over the years.

My work in Chiapas has been strongly supported by Marta Turok, Directora de la Sub-Secretaria de Culturas Populares, who first introduced me to design symbolism; M. Teresa Pomar and Ruth Lechuga of the Museo Nacional de Artes Industrias Populares del Institutio Indegenista have given me their personal support as well as institutional backing; Irmgard Johnson tried without success to make me cautious; Patricia Anawalt shared her knowledge of Pre-Columbian costume; Amber Past resurected natural dyes in Chiapas; Francesco Pellizi supported the collection of Chiapas textiles and encouraged my research and writing; Robert Laughlin helped me, among other things, to receive funding from the Smithsonian Institution; Susanna Ekholm of the New World Archaeological Foundation sponsored and oversaw my research on Classic Maya costume and weaving techniques; and George Stuart encouraged my study of Pre-Columbian textile designs published by the National Geographic Society. Dee Smith of InterCultura has helped me organize a number of exhibitions of Sna Jolobil's weavings over the years, as has Louis Casagrande of the Science Museum of Minnesota. Clare Smith of Aid to Artisans and Ted MacDonald and Lydia Leon of Cultural Survival all endorsed my work with Sna Jolobil. The John D. and Catherine T. MacArthur Foundation refuses to reveal who sponsored my Fellowship Award, which included five years of generous support.

I dedicate this book to Marla Hooks, whom I love.

W.F.M., Jr.

I would like to express my sincere gratitude to the many individuals who made this book possible. Peter J. Ketchum and William Hubbell gave me the opportunity to develop as an ethnographic photographer. A. J. Saunders supported me in every phase of my life. Chip Morris generously shared with me his rapport in the Tzotzil-speaking communities, which in many cases was the only way these photographs could be made. John Burstein, "Tzotzilologist," was my first guide to Zinacantan in 1977. Christiana Dittmann worked with me on my first trip to Chiapas; we shared the thrill of discovering that place. Cristina Taccone, a gifted photographer, assisted me on several expeditions. Dr. Louis B. Casagrande, Curator of Anthropology at the Science Museum of Minnesota, arranged the funding for two trips, and Melissa Mary Ringheim-Stoddard of that museum worked with me on one of the most productive of all my stays. George Stuart of the National Geographic Society and Taylor Greg of National Geographic magazine arranged funding for a photography project on Maya rituals. John Loengard, Todd Brewster, and Mel Scott of Life understood the value of Maya textiles and also arranged for partial funding.

In San Cristóbal, many people have given me support and friendship over the last decade, especially Dr. Robert Laughlin and his wife, Mimi; Susanna Ekholm; Marcy Jacobson and Janet Marin; and Kiki and Gabriel Suarez. Sr. Todoro Maus, cultural attache at the Mexican Consulate in New York; Tomás Goyaneche, Director of INI in Altos Chiapas in 1985; and Teresa Pomar and Ruth Lechuga of the National Museum of Folkart in Mexico City all recognized the importance of this documentation and wrote letters to promote my work. Trudy Duby Blom's photographs gave me a sense of perspective, orientation, and inspiration.

Marti Malovany and Beverly Fazio of Abrams recognized the potential for a book in this material at the opening of the successful exhibition "Time Warps: Mythology in the Weave of the Maya" at the National Arts Club in New York; with Michael Hentges they guided us to the realization of the dream. Marc Mellon, sculptor, Aldon James, president of NAC, and Dee Smith of InterCultura made the exhibit possible. Izzy Seidman, Phil Cantor, and Larry LaBonte were stars on the home team, as was Marc Rousseau, the mechanic behind my mobility; the versatility of my '71 VW camper was essential—at times I thought of myself as a "vanologist" with photographic tendencies.

I feel true friendship in the Maya community with Pedro Meza Meza, his mother, and grandmother; the Tulan family of Nabenchauc, Zinacantan; Mol Domingo of Chamula; Juliana Lopez of Amatenango; and the weavers of Sna Jolobil.

I dedicate this book to the memory of my mother, Helen, who gave me the sensitivity to do this work, and to my father, Philip, who gave me the creative spark.

J.J.F.